Eric Delderfield's

BUMPER BOOK OF

ANIMAL STORIES

Eric Delderfield's
BUMPER BOOK OF
ANIMAL STORIES

DAVID ST JOHN THOMAS PUBLISHER

'I think I could turn and live with animals
    they are so placid and self contained
I stand and look at them long and long,
    They do not sweat and whine about their condition
They do not lie awake in the dark and weep for their sins.'

WALT WHITMAN

British Library Cataloguing in Publication Data
Delderfield, Eric R.
    Eric Delderfield's Bumper Book of True Animal
    Stories
    I. Title
    591

    ISBN 0-946537-76-3

First published 1992
Reprinted 1993

Typeset by XL Publishing Services, Nairn
and printed in Great Britain
by BPCC Wheatons Ltd, Exeter

for David St John Thomas Publsher
PO Box 4, Nairn, Scotland IV12 4HU

— ∞ — ∞ — ∞ — ∞ — ∞ —

Contents

— ∞ — ∞ — ∞ — ∞ — ∞ —

THE THINGS THEY DO

RESCUED AND RESCUERS

ANIMAL FRIENDSHIPS

JUST GOATS

WORLD OF THE HORSE

DOGS – HOW THEY SERVE

— ∞ — ∞ — ∞ — ∞ — ∞ —

Introduction

— ∞ — ∞ — ∞ — ∞ — ∞ —

THIS is my fourth book of true animal stories and once again in gathering them, I am continually astounded at the high degree of intelligence so many of the animals show in special and often hazardous circumstances. Some of the stories which proved most popular in former books have also been included.

We can never begin to understand what makes animals tick. Perhaps the most amazing story is that of the hen that struck up a friendship with a cat. They were boon-companions and then the cat was involved in a fatal accident. Next morning the hen disappeared and was never seen again. There is the story of the intelligence of the labrador who saved his young master's life when the child was up to his arms in sinking sands. Why on earth did Percy the Pirate set himself up as a loner, yet permit an old cat to share in his robberies? And what a sense of self preservation was shown by the spoiled pet cat in existing in the wild, including hazardous traffic, yet survived.

Here are stories of animals in perilous circumstances who kept bright and cheerful as if knowing they would be rescued. A small border terrier down a disused mine shaft for six days and when rescued came up wagging his tail. Then there was Jen, the border collie staying put up a mountain in awful conditions, relying on her master to find her.

Friendship and communication between animals are surely highlighted by the cat which stole golf balls and passed them to his pal to take in the house and hide them, to the chagrin of the players.

9

Goats, in particular, I have found have real personalities with a sense of fun, and then there are the donkeys who look after their sick companions.

Animal friendships are sometimes quite astounding as seen with the duck and the collie, the hamster and the kitten or the alsatian and the tiny goat.

The work that dogs do for the blind and disabled is well known. Also the sometimes hazardous tasks carried out by the police and customs services.

Regrettably so much of all this is offset by the vicious cruelty that so many suffer at the hands of so-called humans.

The whole world seems so full of dreadful stories, mostly due to man's greed. In Africa the high price of elephant's ivory is sounding the death knell of this wonderful and intelligent beast. In the last decade alone ivory poachers have been responsible for decimating half of Africa's total number of this majestic and dignified beast.

The black rhino's horn is worth thousands of pounds to poachers who kill for its mythical value as a phoney aphrodisiac in Africa. Half the total population of these fine beasts in Zambia and Zimbabwe have been poached. But sad to say, not only is cruelty seen in Africa. In this country, in Manchester, 800 cats' paws were dumped in a rubbish skip. It is believed that the poor cats were served up in restaurants.

Dog fighting is still an undercover activity in Britain. Abolished by law in 1935, and in 1987 the penalty for any kind of animal baiting was increased to a maximum fine of £2,000 or up to six months in prison or both. Many feel that the maximum penalty is only rarely, if ever, used. Well might we query how men can watch these courageous animals tear each other to pieces for the 'fun' of a gamble is beyond belief, but like badger baiting it still goes on, though recent parliamentary legislation has brought in stricter surveillance.

Pollution of the rivers and seas is another cause of so much suffering of wildlife.

The RSPCA report that cases of cruelty in Britain have trebled since 1980 and every year they have to put down some 300,000 dogs. Many of these cases are simply because people don't know or care about their pets, once their initial enthusiasm for them is over. But Britain, with a far higher concern for animal welfare than other European countries, is still fighting EC countries over blatant cruelty.

The trade in veal from British calves kept on the continent in 'cruel' conditions has recently come under attack in Parliament. More than 300,000 young calves a year are shipped from Britain to Holland, France and other EC countries where many are fed on restricted diets and reared in cramped cages and artificially-lit sheds.

Despite this method being banned in Britain as cruel, much of the meat is sent back to this country, where it is sold in hotels and supermarkets because it is said to be cheaper.

Britain is, however, the only country in Europe that is vigorously fighting over horses and ponies, battery cages and to abolish veal crates in other countries. The RSPCA wants veal crates banned throughout the EC and all veal calves kept in loose housing arrangements, preferably with wooden slatted floors, and fed proper diets as is required by law in Britain.

Senseless killing goes on in many countries, for instance Malta where the shooting of wildlife passes for sport. Some 14,000 people of a population of 300,000 own licenced guns. Dolphins are considered good practice. Gull fishing, where baited fish hooks are dangled from the cliffs. Gulls swoop to swallow the bait and their insides are torn apart by the sharp hooks. Turtles are kept alive on the sea front to prove that they are fresh to eat. Often they are left thrashing helplessly on their backs for hours on end. Sometimes they are tied by a fin to a mooring and frequently injure themselves trying to escape. An estimated three million finches are trapped on the island each year to spend their lives in tiny cages.

Animals and birds are also a part – and a very pleasing and important part – of this world. Surely with the so-called superior intelligence of man, we can learn to live and let live.

What can we as individuals do about it? The badger legislation has come about by public opinion using pressure on their Members of Parliament. The public can also help by choosing British products and by reporting individual cases of cruelty to the RSPCA (see list of Useful Addresses, p222).

Furthermore we can keep in mind that this country would be a far lonelier place for millions of old people without the love and companionship of their pets.

In these pages there are mostly happy and cheerful stories, showing the sense and courage of animals which often seems to transcend that of humans.

ERD
Exmouth, Devon
1991

— ∞ — ∞ — ∞ — ∞ — ∞ —

THE THINGS THEY DO

— ∞ — ∞ — ∞ — ∞ — ∞ —

— ∞ — ∞ — ∞ — ∞ — ∞ —

Percy the Pirate

— ∞ — ∞ — ∞ — ∞ — ∞ —

IF ever there was a swashbuckling pirate in the guise of a bird – it was Percy.

He was one of the hundreds of gulls that swarm about the pleasant bays and coves of Jersey in the Channel Islands.

He was quite a big fellow and whether or not his bad manners had caused his fellows to ostracise him will never be known, for none ever associated with him – he was certainly a 'loner'.

His first misdemeanour was to alight on the lowest roof of a luxury hotel, situated just inland from the coast, and as regularly as a cockerel, at an early hour, start to screech and squawk. As an early riser himself he did his best to make everyone within earshot 'rise and shine'.

The hotel guests complained bitterly but there was nothing the management could do, Percy was a protected species.

The hotel management did all they could to remove the menace. Three times the RSPCA deposited Percy on the coast of France, but he was always back faster than the boat and settled comfortably on the hotel roof telling all and sundry that he was glad to be home.

His next foray was to watch the milkman on his early delivery leave cartons of yoghurt. Percy watched with interest, then selecting one of the cartons, carried it high above the roadway outside the hotel and dropped it as he did shellfish to crack the shell. The resulting mess in the roadway was quite out of proportion to the size of the carton.

Like all early morning drivers on familiar routes, the motorists drove at maximum speed and often they braked to enter the hotel. It needed just a touch of the brake when a wheel was on the yoghurt to send them into a skid and very often the result was chaos.

Then Percy turned his attention to the hotel dust bins. To tip them over with his weight was child's play and the pickings were always good. In this expedition, strange to say, he had an unlikely ally – a large mangy ginger Tom from a nearby farm. Side by side, he and the bird would feast with gusto and at last satiated they would go their separate ways. Unfortunately for the hotel staff neither of them could read the slogan 'Keep Britain Tidy'.

The hotel management complained vigorously and regularly to the various ministries which guard and guide our destinies. They had a slick answer, 'sea gulls are a protected species', and that was that.

So Percy went his wicked way, plaguing the hotel for three years.

At the hotel in question a courtyard is situated next to the swimming pool divided by a fairly high wall, and one day the management admiring the flowers in the courtyard, spotted a stinking fish head.

Calling down imprecations on Percy, who by now would have been accused of opening the hotel safe and eating all the money, the manager flipped the fish head with his stick and it disappeared over the wall to fall neatly on the bald head of a gentleman guest basking by the pool. Of course Percy was again verbally abused and with some difficulty the guest was placated.

At this stage another appeal was made to the ministry with the same 'no' for an answer.

It was only a day or two later that the same gentleman guest took a dip in the pool, when Percy flew over and no doubt mistaking the military gentleman's sunburnt bald head for a fried egg, swooped at considerable velocity.

The result was both predictable and alarming. Using words not usually heard in a hotel, except perhaps when the steak is overcooked, the guest by now his head pouring with blood demanded action. He was promptly hospitalised.

Again the ministry was appealed to, and by now even their cup of hate was running over. Percy was bad news for tourism, and could no longer be fobbed off as a figment of imagination or heavy consumption of alcohol.

A clandestine expedition next morning was carried out with stealth, bad humour and nervousness but one shot finished the career of 'Percy the Pirate'.

The following day was Sunday and more than the usual number of the hotel guests went to morning service – I wonder why!

— ∞ — ∞ — ∞ — ∞ — ∞ —

Thomas the Terror of Golfers

— ∞ — ∞ — ∞ — ∞ — ∞ —

NORMALLY a black cat spells luck but this is far from the case when members of the Weston-Super-Mare Golf Club approach the fifteenth hole.

No use the players getting excited when they put their ball on the green for their chances of ever seeing it again were remote, for Thomas, a very handsome black kitten of eighteen months was watching.

When the ball lands, out he jumps from the undergrowth behind his garden. Quick as lightning he grabs the ball and runs to his home some 200yd away, where his companion and twin, Oliver, acts as a 'receiver' and runs to open the back door, at which he is adept having practised since he was six months old. Then he takes the stolen ball from Thomas and secrets it away.

The cats belong to Mr and Mrs J. Vezey, whose garden backs on to the golf course.

In twelve months Thomas had collected over a hundred golf balls.

Mrs Vezey and her daughter went to a Cats Protection Society branch having seen some kittens were for sale and went to pick one, though in the end they came away with two, as often happens with soft-hearted people. The tiniest kitten of the litter was all black and was not really expected to survive, but this was the one the daughter chose. It was a poor little scrap which had nothing going for it at all. A tiny, pointed, almost monkey face and a tail like a piece of string which curled round and round so that they expected him to swing from something – again like a monkey. Moreover when he walked, he wobbled. This one was called Thomas. The other one chosen from the litter was named Oliver. At the age of eight months, Oliver started to jump at door handles in an effort to open them and when he failed used the kitchen window as an exit. Practise however made perfect and very soon he became an expert and with one bound could open any door.

Mrs Vezey thinks that Oliver is the brains behind the golf ball robberies and acts as a kind of Fagin while Thomas does the dirty work. He lays out of sight in the bushes and watches Thomas grab the loot, then rushes off to the house, opens the door and puts it safely away.

Mr Vezey is neither amused or proud of the achievements of the two cats. He is reported as saying, 'We've got golf balls in pots, in the wardrobe, in chests and even under the bed. I'm sick of it but what can we do for there is no way of stopping them.'

The cats are an unbeatable team and on a busy day they will retrieve a dozen balls before lunch.

The secretary of Weston-Super-Mare Golf Club said the cats have a particular yen for yellow balls which cost around £1.60 each.

The owner of the cats has offered two balls for every one

lost, but strange to say, there are few callers.

On lean days, the cats bring in shrews and field mice, and once a tiny kitten.

Both Thomas and Oliver are now handsome animals and are great fans of snooker which they watch avidly on television.

— ∞ — ∞ — ∞ — ∞ — ∞ —

Cat Out in the Cold

— ∞ — ∞ — ∞ — ∞ — ∞ —

THE perceptivity of cats is always amazing as is the range of expressions they can turn on if offended.

There was, for instance, a fine ginger-and-white cat who like the rest of his tribe was fond of his comfort and always chose a sheepskin rug in front of the fire for his snooze.

On one occasion the family went away for a long winter weekend and by mistake turned off the central heating.

On their return instead of a joyful victory roll inside the front door, there was no cat to be found. A room to room search was to no avail. Calls and rattling of a tin which usually brought him at a run failed. So a more careful room to room search was organised, and then in front of the fireplace ensconced *under* the sheepskin rug a head appeared, and to say the cat glared is an understatement. The tip of her tail, the only other part of her body to be seen, waved frantically. Her face told all – 'fancy leaving me in a cold house'. Days passed before she became friendly again.

— ∞ — ∞ — ∞ — ∞ — ∞ —

Cat and Dog Life

— ∞ — ∞ — ∞ — ∞ — ∞ —

THE previous book of animal stories included the story of Dusky, a border collie. Alas, he died after giving more than eleven years of loyalty and joy to so many people.

His replacement (Dusky II) was a bitch of the same breed and almost identical in colour and marking, but she had been in two other ownerships before and the 'boss' felt sorry for her – it was a mistake. Something in her past had terrified her and she proved trainable only to a point.

Heavy lorries particularly were anathema to her and after a while it was decided she had had some awful experience on a motorway. As a guard dog she was superb but once callers were inside the house she would go quiet with a look on her face as if to say, 'If it's alright with you boss, it's alright with me'.

When she had only been with her new master a week and still on a lead, they stopped one morning in the town square where she had never been before. A Norwegian band of some fifty players were assembled to give a concert. They were all in view except the conductor, the sight of whom was obscured by a tree. Suddenly he raised his baton and the band crashed into a march. The sound was both sudden and deafening to both man and dog. Terrified she slipped her collar and was off through the crowd like a shot, she jumped a wall and fled through streams of main road traffic without mishap.

With a friend, the 'boss' searched all over the town for hours – no dog! As a last recourse the searchers went to the sea front, some two miles from the town and a mile from her

20

home, where she had been a few times and it was in the complete opposite direction to the town.

There she was found sitting patiently. It was just another example of the 'compass' inside a dog's head and this wonderful instinct animals have for direction.

Dusky's two hates were postmen and council dustcarts. No matter where she was in any part of the country she could spot a postman way in front and nothing would stop her barking until her quarry was out of sight.

The time came, however, when progressively she became too possessive and anyone touching or even going too close to her boss made her snap. It was an attitude that even extended to the lady of the house and in the end she had to be put to sleep before real trouble ensued.

It was strange that whilst never exactly eager she would grudgingly go into the vets, but on the fatal day she slipped her collar and ran off down the road. When eventually she did get into the surgery she gave a most haunting look as if she knew. Perhaps she did.

Dusky's companion at home was a handsome black-and-white cat with a fine set of three-inch long white whiskers, a white front and white feet, gorgeous owl-like green eyes and a sleek, shiny black coat. She so wanted to be friends with the dog and made many overtures but it was a case of thus far, no further, and a kind of armed neutrality came into being. If the cat was tried too far, then she would turn – claws extended and Dusky quickly decided that discretion was the better part of valour and ran off howling.

Dusky's demise left Topsy the cat king of the castle. For a few days she seemed to mope and search for the dog and then after a week took over Dusky's role. Wherever she is, the whistle of just one particular tune will bring her hot foot and she knows the time of the after lunch snooze to a decimal point. She will take a running jump on to the boss's knees, curl up and sleep. The same in the evenings. Once there however, she resents being disturbed particularly if it means total inconvenience to attend to the television. Her pupils will go into slits and very plainly she will show her feelings by sitting with her back to everyone and licking herself, at the same time really scowling. She will put up with being moved once and even a second time but being disturbed three times is more than she can stand. Alternatively she may come back three times but then touch her if you dare. Her lovely round eyes will again narrow into mere slits – her tail will lash about and out come the claws.

She will respond to the whistle without fail, but sometimes if curled up somewhere she decides to come but shows all and sundry she is no dog, by taking four or five steps then stopping to groom herself as much as to say, 'I'm coming, but in my own time'.

The owner always found with all his animals that just one tune would bring them to him and that was *Coming Round the Mountain* – no other substitute, even *Abide with Me*, would work. It had however a happy sequel for a famous artist, Sarah-Leigh Williams, was intrigued with this and for a present to the owner painted a superb picture of a mountain with a train going round it and a waterfall beside it down which descended tins of 'Whiskas'. In front of this background was Topsy in full glory.

It is always a pleasure to watch her when the week's shopping is deposited on the kitchen table. Like an official taster for the king in medieval days she puts her head in every bag and sniffs at every package. Then and only then will she drop gracefully to the floor as much as to say, 'It's okay now, you can put the stuff away'.

All cats are self-centred and wonderfully patient and invariably end up getting their own way. They relax so gracefully and I can always understand the Egyptians making them objects of worship. What's more I can understand the cats graciously accepting such homage.

— ∞ — ∞ — ∞ — ∞ — ∞ —

Belle's Curiosity

— ∞ — ∞ — ∞ — ∞ — ∞ —

THERE are a multitude of stories of how curiosity have nearly, but not quite, killed the cat. The felines are certainly tough when it comes to hanging on to life.

An instance was Belle who crawled under floorboards when builders were fitting new floorboards in a house at Ross-on-Wye. Belle crawled underneath and went exploring among the joists. Quite unaware that they had a visitor, the carpenters nailed down the new boards.

The owners had missed their three-year-old cat and given her up for lost when they heard that a cat had been found nearby. A woman had been polishing the new floor when she heard faint purrs coming from underneath. They lifted the boards and sure enough out crawled Belle.

She was in a terrible state and only weighed a few ounces. She had been imprisoned there for twenty-three days, obviously without food or water.

The cat was nearly blind and terrified, but taken home, she started to eat and was soon on her way to a complete recovery.

One wonders how she managed to survive at all.

— ∞ — ∞ — ∞ — ∞ — ∞ —

I am indebted to a reader for the story about two cats – names unknown – who were great pals. One went missing for several days and the other searched high and low and eventually found her companion and proudly led it home again. Whatever their names were, it was a natural that they were promptly renamed Stanley and Livingstone.

— ∞ — ∞ — ∞ — ∞ — ∞ —

Firemen to the Rescue

— ∞ — ∞ — ∞ — ∞ — ∞ —

FIREMEN get many unusual calls from humans and also occasionally for animals, and typical of these was the occasion when Mick, a border collie who was blind, needed help. An Exeter family had had him for twelve years and he lost his sight in the last three years.

One morning his mistress was talking to a neighbour, who also had a dog, and Mick came out to chat up the visiting dog and to get as close as possible pushed his head through the wrought iron gate. When he tried to withdraw his head he found it jammed. Every effort was made to free him, but poor chap, he was no help as he got very confused and upset.

So the Fire Brigade was called. They were quick, kind and considerate and used bolt croppers to cut the iron.

Naturally Mick was badly shaken up, but soon recovered and became his usual self.

— ∞ — ∞ — ∞ — ∞ — ∞ —

Rescue for a Kitten

— ∞ — ∞ — ∞ — ∞ — ∞ —

TIED to a brick and thrown into the river at Isleworth, Middlesex, Sooty, a five-day-old kitten, was scooped out caked with mud and gasping for life by an RSPCA inspector.

But there was a silver lining. The resultant publicity led to more than 200 telephone calls, some from as far away as Wales and Liverpool, offering the kitten a home. The inspector was later awarded the RSPCA bronze medal for the rescue.

— ∞ — ∞ — ∞ — ∞ — ∞ —

Squirrel De-bags a Postman

— ∞ — ∞ — ∞ — ∞ — ∞ —

IT sounds quite unbelievable, but a squirrel was responsible for a Devon postman being caught with his trousers round his ankles and his pride quite devastated.

The postman was driving his van on a fairly lonely road across a common when he spotted a small squirrel sitting, bushy tail up, in the centre of the road. A hoot on the horn had no effect, so he brought his vehicle to a halt and went to investigate.

To the man's amazement the bushy, tailed rodent was not a bit put out. The postman then bent down to lift the little fellow clear and at last it moved – at lightning speed – and ran up inside the young man's trouser leg. Efforts to dislodge the squirrel failed and the petrified man, fearing it might try and bite its way out, hastily lowered his trousers. In his predicament and standing in his pants he was still trying to dislodge his unwelcome guest when a woman motorist drove by, and more by luck than judgement managed to keep control of her steering wheel.

The postman by now as red as a beetroot struggled into his trousers and re-zipped but still the little rodent refused to go. At last the man decided to get back to his van lest the little beastie should explore his other leg. But obviously it longed for company so it perched on the wheel of the van. This time a blast on the horn did dislodge the intruder and off it skipped to the woods.

By now, very late on his round the postman eventually got back to the post office where, when he had finally convinced his mates it had not been a dream, he became the butt of their humour – something which will obviously continue for some time.

Perhaps the squirrel also went back to his mates, and probably asked them the meaning of all the four-letter words he had heard.

— ∞ — ∞ — ∞ — ∞ — ∞ —

An Honorary MP

— ∞ — ∞ — ∞ — ∞ — ∞ —

THE life of a guide dog to the blind is normally fairly humdrum, but for sheer boredom that of Offa, who sits patiently through the business, debates and question time in the House of Commons, takes the biscuit.

He is owned by Mr David Blunkett, the Member of Parliament for Sheffield Brightside, who is blind.

His first dog, Ruby, was only permitted to go into the House of Commons after a considerable battle with the authorities in 1970 and was the first dog ever to be allowed into the Palace of Westminster. Mr Blunkett's next dog was Teddy who accompanied his master everywhere and after his lamented death in 1988 was followed by the present Offa, a golden retriever, German Shepherd cross, often seen by viewers when the House is being televised.

Sympathy must be extended to the poor animal to have to put up with an atmosphere that sometimes makes a jungle seem quiet. After all the humans *seek* the job.

Only once was Offa mildly disgraced himself when he brought up his breakfast during a debate on the Poll Tax.

The House of Commons is vast with a succession of wide corridors, and with masses of people milling about it does not make navigation easy, but Offa only has to receive a command 'find the door' or 'find the lift' and without hesitation he leads his master to them.

Sad to relate in 1991 Offa was injured in a road accident, just hours after Offa and his master had attended the State Opening of Parliament.

Mr Blunkett and his dog were crossing a main road in Sheffield when the dog was hit by a van.

Unfortunately the people who reported the accident left him on the pavement and went to the pub. When the police arrived Offa had stumbled away. It appeared that a firework being let off in close proximity upset him. It took a further ten hours to find him.

His owner who is Shadow Local Government Minister and MP was overjoyed to have him returned. The dog was badly cut and bruised and in shock but with careful nursing was soon on the mend and back on his job within two weeks.

— ∞ — ∞ — ∞ — ∞ — ∞ —

Dog Earned His Dinner

— ∞ — ∞ — ∞ — ∞ — ∞ —

MR J. Vowles who runs the sub-post office at Newton Row, Birmingham, England, has as his constant companion, for both social and security reasons, a handsome black alsatian with sable markings who rejoices in the official pedigree name of Aston Ritter. This is rather too much of a mouthful, so from an early age he has been known simply as Dog.

Dog is a well adjusted animal, extremely fond of children, and even though he is now nine years old ever ready for a game. But he knows to a nicety how many beans make five and does not confuse a game with the fierce tussle of life. That he can tell the difference between those who enter the shop to buy and those who come in with a more sinister purpose in mind was made quite clear one summer morning recently when he accompanied his master to the shop as usual.

Mr Vowles was on his own and Dog was reclining behind the counter. Suddenly two men burst into the shop demanding money. Dog came to life with a vengeance, leapt up snarling and was at the intruders like a shot. They turned tail and fled, with the alsatian on their heels, making for a get-away car parked outside. They drove off, a witness said, as if the devil was after them. The whole episode was over so quickly that Mr Vowles hardly saw the raiders. He did not know whether they had been bitten or not, but he was quite sure that on this particular day Dog really had earned his dinner.

A Tale of Two Cats

TIGER Tim, a magnificent young cat, was ginger-and-white and lived one side of the road. Boots, a handsome, patriarchal cat, was black-and-white – his paws were startling white, hence his name – and he lived on the opposite side of the road. The two were on nodding terms as neighbours but when either of their owners went away the cats became lodgers in each other's houses.

Tiger Tim, as became his age, was playful. Boots, on the other hand was dignified and would usually pass by majestically when the younger cat took a swipe at him with his paw. Periodically he would enter the contest, but even then no fur would ever fly. It would not be a serious confrontation and, like boxers sparring in the ring, would take place with an entire absence of spite or venom.

Such occasions remind us that felines have their own very real personalities. When the sparring commenced Boots would immediately take up a vantage point on a chair, and Tiger would attack, the bout going on for perhaps ten minutes. Boots would disdainfully wave a paw, with a look on his face which plainly said, 'I am the king of the castle and I intend to remain so without undue effort'. Finally, after repeated sorties, Tiger Tim would spring and obtain a foothold on the chair and Boots, calmly omnipotent, would place a giant paw on his head and by sheer weight push him down. Thus the contest ended until next time.

Neither animal would ever steal or muscle in on the other's food. Tiger, in fact, never attempted to touch anything left within reach; but Boots was otherwise an incorrigible thief – nothing was sacred, not even the Sunday joint, and never did his eyes prove bigger than his massive stomach.

On one occasion Tiger's strange behaviour astonished all who saw it. From a window in the house he was observed jumping up and down on the grass with his four feet spread-eagled. Up and down like a yo-yo he went, eyes blazing and whiskers quivering. Closer inspection revealed an adder on the lawn, its writhings and turnings beating time as it were to Tiger's jumps. On the touch-line in magnificent isolation was Boots, watching every move. After a while the snake was decapitated with a spade. Its writhings continued but Tiger, just as if he knew that all was safe, ceased his sparring. Boots now frankly bored, moved off. Never having seen a snake before, how did Tiger know he had met a dangerous foe, for there was no mistaking his demeanour?

One day a third, very elderly cat joined them. He belonged to a poor, old lady and had been her constant and only companion. Until a good home had been found for him, she had refused to be moved to hospital and, judging by his good condition, he seemed to have had more than his fair share of the available food. Poor old Micky was content to lie sleeping all day, but any sudden movement would terrify him. It was quite a time before it was realised that this was probably due to the fact that he had never been used to anyone moving quickly – his aged and crippled mistress had for years perforce moved very slowly.

When Micky first arrived, Tiger and Boots duly inspected him. After that, the two younger cats were never again seen to approach the new visitor. They seemed to size up the situation at once and to mutually agree that here was one to whom they must be charitable, that Micky was old and tired and that they should let him sleep peacefully.

Sad to say, Micky's mistress died a few weeks later and, not long afterwards, as if in sympathy, he followed her.

— ∞ — ∞ — ∞ — ∞ — ∞ —

Caroline the Camel

— ∞ — ∞ — ∞ — ∞ — ∞ —

JACK Aspinwall, Member of Parliament for Wansdyke, always loved animals and when he was asked to ride Caroline the camel, jumped at the chance. Caroline and Mr Aspinwall entered Sports Aid (the Race against Time) to raise money for children's charities at home and abroad.

Luckily, Lord Bath lent Caroline to Sports Aid and allowed the 'eager rider' to take her for a 'test run' at Longleat. Mr

Aspinwall's impressions, as can well be imagined, were rather sore ones. A camel is not the most gentle of creatures when it decides to stand up, nor when it gets going for that matter, and Caroline, the nineteen-year-old dromedary, proved no exception. The sensation of actually riding a camel is rather like being tossed at sea. Mr Aspinwall learnt that a camel is also a technical term for a machine which adds buoyancy to vessels and that just about sums it up!

At least the 10km ride was nothing like the normal camel train distance in Africa. Camel drivers have to be adept at the subtle art of 'hobbling' which for the benefit of non-camel drivers is a way of tying their front legs together so that the long suffering beasts do not run away in the night.

Mr Aspinwall noticed that Caroline had soft widespread two-toed feet to enable her to walk on sand and snow in her native land. When she ran, her legs on each side moved in unison producing a characteristic pacing gait – which is not the most comfortable of movements. Camels also have double rows of protective eyelashes, hairy ear openings and the ability to close the nostrils in order to adapt themselves to unfavourable situations. At least the Lansdown Playing Fields in Bath had nothing like that to offer.

Mr Aspinwall added, 'Although docile when properly trained and handled the beasts can be prone to fits of rage, in particular during the rutting season. They spit when annoyed and can bite. This I learnt to my peril and whilst rather taken by Caroline I did not think she was overly impressed with me. When I turned to discuss tactics with her keeper she took a nip at my back – rather like political opponents or is it colleagues. I can never quite tell!'

On the race day itself things went fairly smoothly. The novice rider managed to ride Caroline for five laps but the large crown began to agitate her. Not wanting to risk landing on his derrière in front of thousands of constituents – not quite the dignified display he had in mind – he decided to walk with her for the rest of the track.

By early evening Caroline and her new rider completed

their task. Whilst Caroline retired to her bed at Longleat, Mr Aspinwall adjourned home to bathe his wounds and to lie on his stomach as he dreamt of Lawrence of Arabia, camel coats and caravans.

— ∞ — ∞ — ∞ — ∞ — ∞ —

A Cat's Twelve Mile Walk

— ∞ — ∞ — ∞ — ∞ — ∞ —

A farm cat which lived in a barn got into the habit of waiting for the milk churns to be collected and one day when the milk lorry came to collect he went missing. The lorry went on its way on a very circular route and at the end of its collections churns were rolled off at the depot, revealing a cat laying snugly between the last three cans. The cat had no intention of being caught and jumped off.

Fortunately the lorry driver remembered seeing the cat on his first call and told the cowman the next day. There was however, nothing they could do and regretfully they gave up hope of seeing him again.

Fifteen days later, the cat limped into his former home. It had come some twelve miles and could not possibly have seen anything from the lorry. Its paws were bleeding and it was starving but it made it.

This direction finding often occurs. How do animals manage it?

The cat's lifestyle changed and no longer does he live in the barn. As if to say enough is enough he took up residence in the cowman's house where his paws were tended after his long walk, and what is more, he does not go near the milk lorry.

— ∞ — ∞ — ∞ — ∞ — ∞ —

Maggie May Likes Her Pint!

— ∞ — ∞ — ∞ — ∞ — ∞ —

THERE was once a Welsh pony who was put up for sale at Barnet Fair in Hertfordshire. Sold and repurchased, the mare was in due course in foal to an Appaloosa stallion and at this period was purchased by someone in Kent. A fine foal was born, and was named Maggie May.

Alas, very soon afterwards the mother was killed in a road accident and Maggie had to be reared by hand. Such a start in life did not make the foal robust. But lean and skinny though she was, she caught the eye of Mr Fred Chilmaid who had started livery stables at Bean, near Dartford in Kent. He purchased her and she joined the rest of them at the stables.

Maggie May soon showed a love for human company, especially that of children, and quickly established an attachment to Gillian, the nine-year-old daughter of the licensee of the local public house, the 'Royal Oak'. And so it was that Maggie May was allowed into the bar one day when Mr Chilmaid called for a pint. Maggie was not only curious, but apparently envious as well, and she avidly licked a finger dipped into the beer and made obvious signs for more. So she acquired the taste and now, with her own tankard, she has her daily pint as a matter of course.

Maggie May is now two years old and beloved by all around. Mr Chilmaid has promised her to the daughter of another licensee at the 'Rising Sun' in Northfleet, but will continue to stable her. So Maggie May will be able to keep up the invigorating custom of 'wetting her whistle'!

— ∞ — ∞ — ∞ — ∞ — ∞ —

Six Years Away and Home Called

— ∞ — ∞ — ∞ — ∞ — ∞ —

ANOTHER amazing case of the homing instinct of cats comes from a lady in Chard, Somerset.

Tigger was a family pet who was a home lover, but after eating his festive dinner at Christmas 1985 just disappeared. After much searching and heartache they had to accept his loss. In due course the family obtained another cat called Max.

In September 1991 a neighbour saw a cat sitting on her fence and said that it looked very much like Tigger, the missing one. So the family went to look for themselves and sure enough it was the wanderer returned, for the cat was identifiable by some scars on its nose.

Tigger used to enjoy sitting in the car and it is believed that someone must have driven off not realising that the cat was there, and he had been finding his way home ever since.

The well travelled cat settled back in his home as if he had never been away and moreover has been accepted by Max, his successor.

— ∞ — ∞ — ∞ — ∞ — ∞ —

A Bull Goes Walkabout

— ∞ — ∞ — ∞ — ∞ — ∞ —

A one-ton bull named Pegasus got bored in his field in Derbyshire and decided to seek pastures new. The four-and-a-half-year-old pedigree animal, as a first step, savaged the field gate, then went walkabout. This led him through a cottage garden where he crashed open the kitchen door.

Crossing the kitchen, Pegasus then entered the utility room and smashed the front of the gas boiler by sitting on it. He then moved on to the bathroom.

Having destroyed the shower room glass door, he wrecked the lavatory bowl and the wash basin. But at least he smelled good because he inadvertently doused himself with after-shave.

But his decision to take a look out of the window ended his rampage, for there he became stuck and remained so until the police were called and they then contacted the bull's owner. The owner of the cottage discovered his troubles were not over, for to free the bull the bathroom wall had to be demolished.

Surveying the £1,000 damage the owner said, 'I was pretty upset at first but I can see the funny side of it now. He would wreck the one room that didn't need decorating!'

Pegasus was led meekly home after his whirlwind trip which created so much damage.

THE THINGS THEY DO

— ∞ — ∞ — ∞ — ∞ — ∞ —

Inborn Instinct

— ∞ — ∞ — ∞ — ∞ — ∞ —

THE way in which dogs of certain breeds show their hereditary traits at an early age is fantastic. This is particularly noticeable in sheepdogs such as border collies.

One such, Dusky, born near a Cotswold farm, was collected at the age of three months by his new owner who lived near Exeter. Getting him back to Devonshire by car presented a few problems. The pup was small enough to be put into a cat basket, but he was obviously going to be a character and keeping him there was another story. His new boss was negotiating the steep gradient of Cleeve Hill, Cheltenham, when the pup decided he would like to make closer acquaintance; so he climbed out of the basket, scrambled over the seat and up on to the driver's shoulders. Pushed down, he then explored the floor of the car, made a puddle, curled up and went to sleep, in which blissful state he remained for the next three-and-a-half hours, only waking when his new home was reached. He was soon very active and grew fast, travelling some 500 miles a week all over the country in the car with his master.

His first adventure with sheep took place on the wild Yorkshire moors beyond Hawes, when he was still very young. He was let out of the car for a stretch and within seconds was away. Right to the top of the moor he went, not pausing as he climbed the steep inclines to a height of about 250ft. From the road he had spotted sheep running free on the hillside, and it was only a matter of minutes before he had rounded them up and was driving them before him. Fortunately his direction ran parallel with the road, so his

36

bewildered owner drove along trying to keep level. Even at that early age he had been trained to return from short distances when the car hooter sounded, but this time he ignored the call. The thrill of the job was really in his blood. For about one-and-a-half miles he drove the sheep in a compact mass and had a whale of a time. Then at last two sheep broke away and rushed down to the road. Dusky followed and was caught. The amazing thing is that he had never been face to face with a sheep before, let alone caught their scent.

His owner learnt later in the day that three dogs had been shot during the previous week for chasing sheep. Dusky could well have been the fourth.

— ∞ — ∞ — ∞ — ∞ — ∞ —

A Cat's Excessive Zeal

— ∞ — ∞ — ∞ — ∞ — ∞ —

MITZI is a cat with an aversion to litter and often trailed school children to pick up discarded crisp packets.

She was owned by a probation officer but one day, litter bound, she went too far for she stole two £10 notes and two fivers from a neighbour's house.

Mitzi picked up the notes after getting in through a bedroom window five doors away, then deposited them in the garden of her owner.

A pity that her anti-litter bug cannot be passed on to humans.

— ∞ — ∞ — ∞ — ∞ — ∞ —

They Share a Coat of Arms

— ∞ — ∞ — ∞ — ∞ — ∞ —

BIMBO, a rhesus monkey, made front page news when she escaped from a cage at London's Heathrow airport after arriving in this country. Just as with people, there are animals which never regard prison bars as escape proof. Bimbo played a waiting game and then, when opportunity presented itself, led four of her companions in a break-out after making a hole in the wire mesh of their cage.

Her fellow escapees had not a tithe of Bimbo's skill at evading capture, and all too soon they were back behind bars. Not so Bimbo. For seven months she successfully pitted her animal wits against all that humans and their various aids could do. Many men have been known to receive an award for less spectacular feats.

Possessing all the skill of an escapologist, Bimbo's tactics were extraordinary. In the cargo warehouse at the airport she gleefully took the food that was laid as a bait, and swept gracefully from girder to girder. She would allow keepers to come quite close, then off she would leap, sometimes squatting on the top of her cage and sometimes on a tree just outside the warehouse, but always just out of reach.

Then a new ruse occurred to her. She would hop into her cage, then just as the poor humans thought they had her, would leap out quickly and outwit them once again. She did this several times, but all good things come to an end and she played the trick once too often. Even then the honours went to her, for it was only a drugged dart that eventually slowed her down.

Bimbo's owner is also the owner of Fred, a basset hound.

Fred is another believer in the rights of the individual. One of the delights of his life was to take a morning stroll to Chessington Zoo, where, with the aplomb of a season-ticket holder, he would whisk through the gates and go on a tour. But dogs are not allowed in the zoo and, although this particular one did no harm, rules are rules. Time after time the authorities had to telephone Fred's master and a chauffeur-driven Rolls Royce would be sent to collect him.

At the time that Bimbo and Fred were in the news, their owner, the chairman of the the National Research Development Corporation, was made a life peer; a coat-of-arms was granted to him as Lord Black of Barrow-in-Furness in the County Palatine of Lancaster. And these two animals – the basset hound and the rhesus monkey – were made the two supporters of the coat-of-arms, an unusual distinction. Both have shown zeal and a sense of purpose, so that the motto 'Per Ardua' by hard work – is a fitting tribute.

— ∞ — ∞ — ∞ — ∞ — ∞ —

Cat With Two Names

— ∞ — ∞ — ∞ — ∞ — ∞ —

ANOTHER prime example of the way that cats think things out to their own advantage was when a lady's cat disappeared for three weeks. Baldrick, as he was named, decided to return home but this time with a leg in splints and plaster.

The lady, delighted to see him back, felt so grateful to whoever had taken the injured cat to receive professional attention and made some enquiries to thank whoever was responsible. She found the lady and started to thank her, to be told by the benefactress 'but it's my cat'.

It then turned out that the two ladies had been sharing him for a period of three years. Baldrick received the name after a character in the TV series, *Blackadder*, because he was always in a mess. His name at the other home was Scruffy.

The mystery was then resolved. The cat had visited No 1 home at 6am for breakfast and then after a nap on the lady's bed, made his way back down the street for another meal. At 3pm he returns to the first home for yet another meal.

Presumably the two ladies agreed to let the cunning feline's process continue. One thing the cat could not have been, a weight watcher.

— ∞ — ∞ — ∞ — ∞ — ∞ —

Still Going Strong at 150

— ∞ — ∞ — ∞ — ∞ — ∞ —

BORN in Turkey, once a naval ship's mascot, lived at a Devon Rectory and at least 150 years of age, it is now living in luxury in an historic castle. This has been the experience of a humble tortoise.

Timothy first saw the light of day in Turkey. The Earl of Devon's grandfather owned him, and at some time, about 1880, he was passed on to a naval ship's captain, then stationed in the Mediterranean. Timothy then became a ship's mascot, for how long however, again it is not known, but comfortable and spoiled he undoubtedly was. Ship and tortoise had to part company when the ship was ordered to the Antarctic – definitely not tortoise country.

So Timothy was passed on again and went to live with the Courtenay family at Honiton Rectory in Devon.

In due course when the present Earl of Devon inherited in 1935, Timothy again moved on, this time to Powderham

Castle which has stood on the west bank of the River Exe for nearly 600 years.

The tortoise took up residence in the shrubbery of the castle tower with aplomb.

Since 1880 meticulous records have been kept and he has grown just one-eighth of an inch in the last ninety years, and he is known to be at least 150 years of age.

He happily comes to the call of either Lord or Lady Devon as he knows a tit bit is at hand, or perhaps he is to make a public appearance.

There was such an occasion a few years ago when there was a gathering of American and Canadian Courtenays (the family name) at the Castle. It was during tea on the terrace that Timothy was seen by Lady Devon strolling along a sunken path nearby. She called him back and amazingly he promptly stopped in his tracks, turned and came back to make his way up to the terrace where as a treat he was fed on strawberries. Even a tortoise enjoys the good things of life but on being told, 'that's enough Timothy', he turned away and spotted what he thought was another strawberry. In fact it was the red toe nail of a visitor wearing toe-less sandals. Timothy strolled up and took a nip at the forbidden fruit to the consternation of one person, but to the delight of everyone else.

As winter approaches, Timothy makes his way to the thickest part of the shrubbery to hibernate and sleeps comfortably until about March, when he will reappear but only if he considers the weather suitable.

Timothy has lived peacefully through thirteen reigns, thirty-four Prime Ministers, thirteen major world wars, plus colonial wars.

If he could speak, he would probably tell us that nothing much changes, despite Kings and Queens and Prime Ministers.

Some years ago a companion was brought for Timothy. It was not very much smaller in size but very much younger. The old stager did not seem very excited by the new arrival.

They shared the same dry patch and by their decorous behaviour showed there was more in life than racing around saving time at all costs.

So they existed together for two or three years but alas one day Toby, the newcomer, was found dead. Timothy seemed to take it philosophically and his life goes on as before. He sometimes decides on a longer than usual walk and will be found at a farm up the road – quite a distance for a tortoise.

— ∞ — ∞ — ∞ — ∞ — ∞ —

A runner-up in age was Ali Pasha who was brought from the Gallipoli beaches during World War I. He was found and taken aboard *HMS Implacable* in April 1915 on which Mr Friston was serving.

Ali too became an unofficial ship's mascot and finally went ashore for good at Lowestoft, Sussex, where he lived happily, passed from father to son until a cold virus claimed him in the summer of 1987. He was believed to have been 100 years old.

— ∞ — ∞ — ∞ — ∞ — ∞ —

Geese Go in to Attack

— ∞ — ∞ — ∞ — ∞ — ∞ —

THE hunger of a fox, intent on appeasing his appetite, brought him to an unexpected death when he sought to snatch a goose. He broke into the pen of a gaggle of geese but apparently made history when the geese ganged up and pecked and battered the intruder to death.

It happened in Stratford-on-Avon when the owners of the geese heard quite a commotion at the bottom of the garden.

They guessed it might be a fox trying to break in and when the noise stopped they thought no more about it. Next morning they found the dead fox in the pen. There was just one bite on a goose but the body of the fox was covered in vicious peck marks and wounds.

A spokesman for the RSPB said they had never heard of a similar case and could only assume that the fox was in poor health and too weak to defend itself against the massive onslaught. Normally a fox would have no difficulty in seeing the geese off.

$- \infty - \infty - \infty - \infty - \infty -$

Dog Made His Own Way Home

$- \infty - \infty - \infty - \infty - \infty -$

MR Howard Stevenson, a fifty-eight-year-old businessman, keeps sheep on his smallholding in Nidderdale, near Pateley Bridge, Yorkshire, as a hobby and a relaxation from pressure of other commitments.

In the winter of December 1990 the dales had a heavy fall of snow, along with high winds, causing huge drifts. The drifting continued all morning, so Howard decided to go and open a gate on the moor edge to let his sheep move to lower ground for shelter, his sheep dog Fly accompanied him. He opened the gate and turned to go home, unfortunately a blizzard of 70mph and a chill wind caught him, and walking in two feet of snow, he lost his way and soon realised that to try and make it home was impossible. He stumbled into a drift and it was too deep to clamber out and he knew he must make shelter for himself for the night. He built an igloo of snow balls with his hands and the blizzard obligingly filled in the cracks and then compacted the roof, which was soon covered with snow.

Howard knew he must not go to sleep.

The alarm was raised by his wife Pamela after some hours when he failed to return. A party of neighbours, along with his nineteen-year-old son, set off to go to the gate which they found open but no sign of Howard. They came home and said, 'We just cannot see for it's a hellish blizzard and the wind is back breaking'.

The police were called and it was decided to search early on Sunday.

Police and the Upper Wharfedale Fell Rescue team with tracker dogs organised the search along with approximately eighty friends and neighbours.

Howard knew he must keep awake so talked to himself about his family and prayed, he did not go to sleep and was entombed in his igloo for twenty-seven hours, by which time he was frozen to the ground as he could not move.

The first person to find him was the local gamekeeper, Joe Freeman. Howard was flown to Harrogate hospital and was able to return home in four days. Howard thanks everyone who helped in the operation in any way for his safe return.

He recalls the rescue in every detail.

His dog, Fly, returned home later on her own, hungry but no worse for her ordeal but happy to be with her boss again.

— ∞ — ∞ — ∞ — ∞ — ∞ —

Ocean-Going Goose

— ∞ — ∞ — ∞ — ∞ — ∞ —

WALT Disney's famous little fish that swam and swam right over the dam had nothing on Lucky the goose. Where Lucky came from nobody knows, what went on in that feathered head no one can guess. Perhaps it was just a desire to see the world, perhaps even a goose falls in love; whatever the reason, he took to the water and 'he swam and he swam'. For how long is not known, but by the time the fishing trawler *Norrard Star* came into sight twenty miles off the North Devon coast the goose was hopelessly lost and very exhausted.

Lucky summoned his last remnants of strength and swam alongside the boat where, by means of a net on the end of a pole wielded by the trawler's chief engineer, he was hoisted on to the deck. All in, but still game, Lucky tackled the food provided by the kindly crew and then, warmly settled down in the tackle locker, slept off the gruelling effects of his adventure. Obviously Lady Luck had been on his side.

Lucky was soon waddling about the deck like a trained seaman, but seven days later when the trawler was close to land near her home port, the crew decided to put the goose into the water. Lucky seemed to have had enough swimming and steadfastly refused to leave the side of the boat. So there was nothing for it but to haul him aboard again.

When the trawler finally docked, the problem of what to do with the 'mariner' became acute. Eventually Mr Ingram, the managing director of the company owning the boat, decided to take him home to his children. Their bungalow, almost surrounded by lawn and with two fish ponds, was ideal but, as is often the case on the arrival of an unexpected visitor, some doubling-up was necessary. So the fish were all put into one pond, leaving Lucky to take possession of the other.

The bird was in surprisingly good condition, but so thin he weighed scarcely anything. At first, half a loaf a day plus some pigeon corn formed his diet. Very soon, however, he put on weight and settled for three slices of bread each day plus other tit-bits he could pick up.

Yet another surprise was in store for the rescuers, however. Everyone who professed knowledge of geese had unhesitatingly stated that Lucky was a gander. But after some weeks 'he' surprised everyone by proudly laying twelve eggs. They weighed exactly 8oz each and were so rich that one was sufficient for a large fruit cake.

The goose settled down to a regular routine in her new surroundings. She swam in the pool at the same time every day and then basked in the same spot in the garden. When the master of the house arrived home Lucky could not get there fast enough to greet him. She flew over to him with just her toes touching the ground and he had to stroke and make a great fuss of her before she was satisfied.

There is no question of her intelligence, nor of her inquisitive nature, for she looked inside all the flower pots, inspected the greenhouse, where her visits were disastrous for the young lettuce, and even examined the interior of the car. If the two family corgis did not stand guard over their lunch, she would have that too. Between them there was an armed neutrality dating from the day of her arrival, when she pecked one of them. She disliked the cat, and probably feared it, for she hissed at it whenever it came near.

After some months, Mrs Ingram felt that it was unfair to keep Lucky without company of her own kind, so a companion was obtained. One thing is certain, Lucky is still very much attached to her human family. And, whilst a goose is not an ideal pet to keep in a trim garden where small plants are sacrosanct, the family would not part with her.

— ∞ — ∞ — ∞ — ∞ — ∞ —

Reformed Alsatian

— ∞ — ∞ — ∞ — ∞ — ∞ —

LADY, the seven-year-old alsatian owned by Viv Prince the former drummer of the pop group 'Pretty Things', had a penchant for picking up traffic cones in Sidmouth and at one time there were some thirty in her master's front garden. A council lorry was sent to collect them.

Viv who is a fair-minded man therefore decided he would extend an olive branch to the police by offering Lady's unexpected litter of very beautiful four dogs and one bitch pedigrees to the Devon & Cornwall Constabulary as trainees for he knew they were short of them.

Unfortunately the age of acceptance is twelve months and then only on trial for three months, so they had to be refused.

Therefore when news got round there were scores of offers for the lovely tan, silver and sable grey pups which were soon found homes and placed with individuals.

Viv Prince also has a magnificent real German Shepherd bitch. Prince is the Press Officer for the Raving Loony Green Giant Party which already has one East Devon Council Member in sedate Sidmouth, but his own election address did include a point for dog lovers – more dog wardens in the town and a dog urinal area.

However, Lady and her puppies were not the only centre of attention when Viv Prince decided to object to the Poll Tax in the nicest possible way. He went to the Council Offices with his payment of £46 in 1p and 2p pieces, each carefully counted and wrapped in bags of £1.

The official refused to accept this as payment and after some argument Viv, who was accompanied by his alsatian, became exasperated. Enraged at the ridiculous situation he took out his pocket knife to rip his carefully wrapped copper bags open and mix them up to make the counting even more difficult.

Faced with what she thought was a dangerous man with a big dog and a knife, the clerk pressed the panic button and called the police.

When a policeman arrived he couldn't see why he had been bothered, said the money was legal tender and offered Viv and Lady, who loves cars, a lift back home.

However, you cannot win them all. He was on the sea front with Lady one morning and she had no collar on. He was taken to court, the first to be fined on a bye-law brought in that very day. (Fined £40) + costs.

— ∞ — ∞ — ∞ — ∞ — ∞ —

Traffic Sense of Dogs

— ∞ — ∞ — ∞ — ∞ — ∞ —

IF ever a dog was with it as far as traffic was concerned it is *Spot*, a beautiful black-and-white border collie. In his trip to the town of Totnes in Devon, he seemed to size up the situation. He does various odd jobs like fetching the newspaper, but some time ago decided that a traffic cone had some semblance of authority so he carries his own private cone to town and places it wherever he has to wait.

He also puts it to good use every Tuesday in the summer when the residents go to town dressed up in Elizabethan costumes. On these occasions he goes round collecting money for charity.

— ∞ — ∞ — ∞ — ∞ — ∞ —

In New Zealand, a 16st St Bernard dog must have seen pictures of one of his breed doing rescue work in the Swiss Alps.

Kenworth, a placid four year old, bit a man on the arm in an attempt to stop him stepping on to a busy road. The dog was asleep on the footpath and woke suddenly, saw the man walking into apparent danger and grabbed him by the arm. Kenworth has twice been hit by cars and both times the cars were damaged but not the dog, except for a chipped tooth. From the incidents it is assumed that he knew the road was a dangerous place.

The owner said his dog is always trying to rescue people who are swimming, he just takes them gently by the arm and steers them to the beach.

Unfairly, the owner in this case had to admit the dog bit a man, and he was fined £40.

— ∞ — ∞ — ∞ — ∞ — ∞ —

An Affinity with Caxton!

— ∞ — ∞ — ∞ — ∞ — ∞ —

WE are continually hearing of the queer things birds do. There was the hen, for instance, who fluttered up to the spare wheel under the tail board of a lorry while the driver was at lunch. When he returned he drove right off to Bristol, quite oblivious of the fact that he had a travelling companion taking her first trip. When the bird was discovered, the driver took her up into the cab with him for the return journey, considering it less precarious. The hen showed her gratitude by laying an egg on the seat beside him. The big wide world obviously fascinated the hen, for a week or so later she did the same journey and paid the same price. Her fame will never dim now, for a pub near Bristol has been named after her -'The Travelling Hen'.

Birds nest in the most unexpected places, but quite inexplicable was the choice of a pair of robins who built their nest and reared six youngsters right by the machines in a busy printing works. It happened in a Devonshire town during the Easter holidays, when the robins found that by entering between the louvres high up in the wall, they had the factory to themselves. If they resented the intrusion when the men returned to work, they did not show it. The partly built nest was discovered in what was thought to be a precarious position, so the foreman carefully removed it and fixed it on the top of a 6ft plank, which was stood on end so that it was out of harm's way.

The robins, however, must have had an irresistible affinity with William Caxton for they promptly abandoned the partly built nest and immediately began another at a spot equidistant between three fast running machines and only 4ft above the floor. What is more, they abandoned their first way in and chose an easier one through the open windows. Nest building went on apace, in the corner of a cardboard box and the men put a tray over the top of it for safety. With unabated zeal the birds flew in and out all and every day. Before going direct to the nest, they would alight on one or other of the machines and take stock. Printers' ink worried them not at all, for sometimes they would pause on the inked rollers and every operative had to check carefully before he started up in case the movement should engulf the birds.

Eventually the nest was finished and the hen occupied it. Every morning there was keen competition by the printers to see who could bring the best tit-bits to put on saucers outside the nest. It began to look like a harvest festival. Wars and rumours of wars, strikes and lockouts – all would have taken second place to the well being of the nesting birds. The first enquiry every morning was: 'What's happened – everything all right?'

Then came the morning when the first egg appeared; five more soon followed. The incubation period was a time of great trial to everyone in the building, particularly at one short period when the hen left the nest for some hours. But eventually the eggs were hatched and soon the youngsters made their appearance on trial flights. Sad to say, all did not go well and for some days two or three of the fledglings were missing, to be found later in the boiler room: first one, then others were found dead on the floor. The one fortunate survivor flew off.

So did the parents, but for a day or two only. They returned and started to build a new nest, this time high up in the angle of the metal work of the north-light roof. The printers were worried men. 'What,' they asked, 'will happen when trial flights begin for any new youngsters?' There was a sheer 40ft drop below the nest and no branches to break the fall. They need not have worried, for the birds apparently thought that one out too. Abruptly they stopped the building and started work on a new nest again in a cardboard box, but a little higher than the first nest. It was duly completed; eggs were laid and hatched; and all the processes were again watched over by the humans.

Eventually the fledglings were given flying lessons by the parents, up and down the length of the printing works. One by one in succeeding days they made their exits through the top windows.

The story, however, does not end there. The adult robins still come in for tit-bits, but fly out with them – so the youngsters cannot be far away.

— ∞ — ∞ — ∞ — ∞ — ∞ —

Just a Humble Pigeon, But...

— ∞ — ∞ — ∞ — ∞ — ∞ —

IN London's Leicester Square, one day in the spring of 1970, a passer-by spotted a distressed party; he telephoned the RSPCA and immediately the full weight of the resources of the capital's rescue services went into action – for a pigeon. The bird had apparently become trapped high up in a tree, its leg being entangled in a piece of cord, and for two hours it made futile efforts to free itself.

The RSPCA alerted the fire brigade and five firemen were soon on the spot. Being unable to get their ladder into a point of vantage within the Leicester Square Gardens, they called for more help and soon a 45ft extending ladder from Southwark was speeding to the incident. The appliance was manoeuvred into position and temporary sub-officer David Holland ascended, armed with a net and a knife attached to a pole. Holding the net below the bird, he severed the cord which was trapping the bird, and the pigeon dropped safely into the net. Cheers and clapping from the curious and sympathetic crowd that had inevitably collected greeted the rescue, and these were renewed when the fireman descended the ladder and concluded an eighty-minute rescue operation.

Miss Jean Gilbert of the RSPCA clinic to which the pigeon was taken reported 'nothing broken'; its rescuer could not have been showered with more congratulations had he rescued one of the crowd themselves. It remained for a German visitor who had witnessed the incident to sum it all up: 'This – you could only see it in Britain'.

— ∞ — ∞ — ∞ — ∞ — ∞ —

Over the Cliff and Down the Well!

— ∞ — ∞ — ∞ — ∞ — ∞ —

TO say that the cat and dog of Mrs G R Cheesman are accident prone is to put it mildly. Both of them have had perilous escapes and come through quite unperturbed.

Elsa is a pedigree yellow labrador of the Balrion strain with a lovely face and head and is just over two years of age. She went to dog training class and constantly acted the clown to everybody's amusement, except perhaps that of the trainer.

She has a placid character and nothing much seems to bother her. One day, however, while out walking with her mistress along the cliffs, she ran on ahead and disappeared into some bushes – and just vanished. Whether chasing a rabbit or falling down a cleft will never be known.

After a long search, she was eventually spotted about 100ft below, apparently unconscious on a ledge just a few feet above the vicious jagged rocks below.

A mobile coast guard rescue team was called out to help and one auxiliary was lowered on a rope and was able to reach the dog. By the time the rescuer arrived at the ledge, Elsa had recovered and started to bark excitedly. A harness was slipped round her and man and dog were hauled to safety. It was a miraculous escape and there were no broken bones. All she had to show for her two hour ordeal was a grazed stomach and a swollen tongue where she had bitten it.

Brought to the cliff top, her tail wagged as if it would come off.

Two of Elsa's favourite tit-bits are carrots and oranges. She eats each segment of an orange most daintily with the look of a gourmet, and carrots she simply cannot have enough of them.

Elsa's companion is the family cat Marmie a fine nine-year-old marmalade cat.

One night he too disappeared from the house and as it was so unusual a frantic search was made for him to no avail. Next morning another search was unsuccessful and it was Elsa who eventually led the humans to a dry well which was 30ft deep. Sure enough Marmie was mewing lustily at the bottom where he had been some twelve hours.

A ladder was placed, resting on a beam approximately 15ft below and Mr Cheesman cautiously descended, then transferred the ladder to the lower half of the well. Marmie wasted no time as he scrambled up the ladder like a fireman. At the halfway stage he transferred to his rescuer's shoulder and was brought safely to the top after a twelve hour absence. He was certainly bedraggled but apart from his claws which showed considerable wear, he was as right as rain.

Full marks to Elsa for leading Marmie's rescuer to the well and many marks also to his owner for what must have been a very risky operation.

Little wonder that Elsa's local nickname is wonder dog.

— ∞ — ∞ — ∞ — ∞ — ∞ —

People in the Mass – Ugh!

— ∞ — ∞ — ∞ — ∞ — ∞ —

ANIMALS, like humans, have their likes and dislikes. More often than not, the animal takes decisive steps in the matter and refuses point blank to be a martyr! A fine male tabby cat owned by a family who have a large caravan holiday park in Devonshire did just that.

He arrived when a kitten, as a present for the children, and soon settled into routine. In addition to the three children, there were two handsome alsatians, a brown one named Jasper, and the other black, called Jet. For a year the cat walked about the holiday park, as his fraternity do, poking his nose into everything. He had the run of the house and the farm buildings, and on occasions when the children were a bit too playful or possessive, would make off to the barn and get away from it all by going to sleep in the hay.

As Easter came round in his first year, he was surprised at the great influx of new people. By Whitsun, when the normal population had more than doubled, he found it unbearable and one could almost hear him saying, 'I am not standing for this another year.' Neither did he. When the human deluge commenced next Whitsun he, metaphorically speaking, packed his bag and left. He was away all the summer and no one saw a sign of him. He was written off as lost.

On the day of the first frost, the cat, sleek and well-fed, arrived home. From the children particularly he had a welcome like that of the prodigal son, and in true cat manner he lapped it up, accepted it as no more than his right and graciously consented to settle down for the autumn and winter, claiming as by right the best position in front of the fire.

The following year he treated the arrival, in mild numbers, of touring vans and people for Easter with disdain, but on the Thursday of Whit week he just disappeared again. The family were resigned this time and told themselves he would be back. He was too – at the first frost.

For three years now he has followed the same timetable. No one knows where he goes but he certainly neither wants nor starves. When the holiday park population drops and the air has a seasonal bite to it, they know that 'Johnny will come marching home again'.

Some people do not like cats. This is a cat that only likes some people, and event then in mild doses!

— ∞ — ∞ — ∞ — ∞ — ∞ —

A Surprise Litter

— ∞ — ∞ — ∞ — ∞ — ∞ —

SOPHIE, an old English sheepdog and labrador cross, comes from a tough lineage, for she surprised the Richoux family of Exmouth when she gave birth to a litter of ten healthy puppies.

Sophie had only been with the family for two-and-a-half years and had a lovely gentle and playful disposition. There are three children in the house, Frances, the eldest whose dog it is, Lucie and Eleanor, and it goes without saying they all made a great fuss of four-and-a-half-year-old Sophie's new offspring.

She gave birth to the puppies in the early morning and the first four to be born gave no trouble at all and naturally it was thought that was the total brood. A few hours after the delivery however, Sophie was giving the family concern for she was restless and obviously very much distressed.

After a while therefore she was taken to the vet who discovered the trouble. Another pup – alas dead – was blocking the birth of five more who were safely delivered after a caesarian operation. Whilst the operation is relatively commonplace it is unusual to get any pups behind the dead one out alive. Sophie was lucky and the veterinary surgeon skilful.

Eight of them were black and white and two were entirely black.

Thereafter Sophie perked up and was soon her usual self and proved to be a devoted mum.

Sophie can easily open doors and when she wishes to stretch her legs, simply opens the door with her paw and walks out. On her return she again manages the door handle, so that the only way she can be defeated is by locking the door. Now she attends to her family duties, takes a stroll round the garden, then comes back, somehow counts her brood and then leaves them to gambol or sleep on their own.

Within hours of the story being told in a local newspaper, the telephone rang incessantly and all the pups were found good homes, except the one which the family are keeping.

— ∞ — ∞ — ∞ — ∞ — ∞ —

How Did Rusty Do It?

— ∞ — ∞ — ∞ — ∞ — ∞ —

RUSTY was a young sheepdog, owned by a Devonshire farmer, formerly living at Slapton. He had always enjoyed the complete freedom of farm life, and when the family moved fifty miles across the country to Payhembury village, Rusty went too in the back of the car.

Because it was felt he was likely to wander in the settling down period at his new home, he was confined until he could be taken out. But after a few days Rusty got out on his own and was off. The family searched for him in vain, until they heard from the police that he had arrived at their former home at Slapton.

It is difficult to imagine what happened on that lonely journey when he must have felt that every man's hand was against him. From Payhembury, he would probably have gone along the busy A30 road which in the season carries practically non-stop traffic, and even in the quieter months is always busy. Then as he approached Exeter, he would have felt confused, just as a country-born human being would be when faced with a city jungle for the first time. Nevertheless, somehow Rusty, by what trial and error, by what fruitless march and counter-march we shall never know, must have crossed the city and found himself on the A30 again, with the Torquay and the Plymouth traffic flashing by. Which way did he head then? Along the River Exe to Newton Abbot? Did he stick to the main road or did he perhaps keep to the byways until he struck his former home?

It is heart breaking to think of the many bitter disappointments he must have experienced, of his many escapes from the traffic, of his search for food. How far did he really travel to cover that fifty miles – 100 or 200 miles? Many breeds of dogs can travel forty, even fifty miles in a day's work, but poor old Rusty took a fortnight. Only his dejected and physical condition on arrival can tell us a tiny part of the real story. He was wild, unkempt, very thin, and his pads were in a bad state.

When his owners were notified of his arrival, they collected him, overjoyed at his return to Payhembury. For just nine days he seemed content to be home, but he must have found the new non-farming life strange for suddenly he disappeared once more, and sad to say was never heard of again.

— ∞ — ∞ — ∞ — ∞ — ∞ —

Monty Taken to the Cleaners

— ∞ — ∞ — ∞ — ∞ — ∞ —

MONTY is a handsome five-year-old colour point Persian cat who is idolised by the Bastin family – especially by sixteen-month-old Laura.

The cat might have been just looking for adventure one morning, or more probably forty winks in the warm to take the chill off our English summer. Whatever she was searching for he certainly found the unexpected. He was the pet of a busy family of a doctor, his wife and three children and no one noticed that Monty had strolled into the garage and after nosing round for a while, as cats do, settled himself inside the tumble dryer. He must have been surprised when a little later, some bed sheets were piled in on top of him.

Then the machine was switched on and it was not until thirty-five minutes later and thousands of revolutions that the machine was stopped and out came the bed sheets – and the poor cat!

He was quite goggle-eyed, his tongue hanging out and naturally running a very high temperature.

Fortunately Dr Bastin was in the house and quickly took charge. He took some ice cubes from the fridge to cool the cat who was steaming like a suet pudding. This attempt was not very successful, so he unceremoniously doused the cat in water and then put him out on the verandah, wrapped in a towel to dry.

Mrs Bastin said they had heard a different rumble in the machine which gradually got worse, so her husband went to the garage to investigate – there was a clonking and a meek meowing.

They say cats have nine lives and certainly this was a minus one for Monty. In a day or two the cat was as right as rain and back in the bosom of his family – being fussed over by Joel ten, Simon twelve, and Laura who follows him everywhere.

He has taken up his former mode of life but understandably will not go near the garage.

— ∞ — ∞ — ∞ — ∞ — ∞ —

Rocky on the Rocky Mountain

— ∞ — ∞ — ∞ — ∞ — ∞ —

SIXTEEN-year-old Gareth Davies was deeply attached to his two-year-old terrier and when they were out rabbiting on the mountainside near Merthyr Tydfil, near Glamorgan, one winter day, Rocky, a border terrier, suddenly disappeared down a hole and, as was later discovered, fell some 40ft, where he landed on a ledge.

The RSPCA were quickly notified and a rescue team arrived under the direction of an Inspector. They worked for a long time in dreadful conditions, rain, snow and a bitter cold, damp atmosphere.

They could hear the dog barking, but could not see him and threw down dog meat and their own sandwiches to keep him going.

The first operations were taken with great care in case they should cause a fall of rock on to the trapped animal. Soon they had to send for heavy drilling equipment to get through the rock. In conditions prevailing it was hard and slow work.

Eight days later, Mr M Townsend, a friend of the dog's youthful owner, went up to see how things were proceeding and decided he would squeeze through the hole taking only a torch and a rope. It was naturally a very hazardous operation, but he managed to get to a ledge within 10ft of the terrier. He then threw down a sandwich and as the little dog went to eat it he threw down a rope with a noose at the end. In a remarkably lucky throw he managed to lasso the terrier and quickly hauled him up to the ledge and then made his precarious climb to the top.

He carried the dog down the mountainside to be re-united with his master. The small animal did not have a long tail, but he made the most of what he had and wagged it furiously, giving his boss a thorough and joyous licking.

While the terrier was found to have lost a great deal of weight he was otherwise unharmed and ate ravenously from a plate of corned beef, tripe and biscuits with a bowl of milk which was his homecoming feast.

Rocky's eight days of ordeal were over and never again will he be taken to the same spot for exercise.

The RSPCA Inspector said it had been an expensive operation in overalls, safety harness and tools but was delighted to know that the dog was safe.

— ∞ — ∞ — ∞ — ∞ — ∞ —

Rescued and Rescuers

— ∞ — ∞ — ∞ — ∞ — ∞ —

— ∞ — ∞ — ∞ — ∞ — ∞ —

Whale Says Thank You

— ∞ — ∞ — ∞ — ∞ — ∞ —

AGAINST the stories of horrible cruelty and neglect of animals we came across heartening stories of magnificent courage and care for creatures of the wild.

One such was that of the 30ft whale which by some mischance ran aground on rocks off the Cornish coast. It was a rare Fin Whale which became trapped by the ebbing tide after swimming into the bay at Mousehole. The marine giant thrashed around in a gully with no likely hope of escape. It was then that three lifeboat men joined by RSPCA and conservation inspectors decided to attempt a rescue. After several attempts they were able, by almost a miracle, to get a rope under the tail of the whale. The ground swell came in and lifted her and because of the hold on her tail she turned with her head to the sea but when she saw it they quickly undid the rope and shouted. The sea picked her up and she went down two fathoms. The sea picked her up again, she blew her water hole then amazingly came back towards the rescuers as if to say thank you, blew her water hole again and went off at speed into the bay.

By now a crowd had collected on the cliff top and they cheered hysterically as the whale put out to sea.

It is believed that the whale's brain is as big as a human's and it would certainly seem like it from this story.

— ∞ — ∞ — ∞ — ∞ — ∞ —

Bruce, Hero of the Mudflats

— ∞ — ∞ — ∞ — ∞ — ∞ —

A handsome nine-year-old black labrador with a little alsatian in him is the hero of this story.

Four-year-old Spencer James, whose home at Monkton,
Pembrokeshire, is near the river, wandered down to the water
at low tide one morning with Bruce, a neighbour's dog, and
became trapped in the morass of mud left by the receding
water. It was not long before the boy was in difficulties,
sinking until he was up to his armpits. Only his head and the
top of his shoulders were clear, when Bruce, with amazing
understanding, quickly summed up the situation. Lying on
his side, he took hold of one of the boy's shoulders to prevent
him sinking further. No one knows how long he played this
heroic supporting role; it might have been ten minutes or half
an hour.

Meanwhile, Spencer's mother had missed him and had
searched for him in all his usual haunts. Hearing cries from
the direction of the river, she hurried there to see the boy out
in the channel with Bruce holding on to his shoulder.

Spencer was rescued and his mother lost no time in getting
him into a hot bath. It was then that the grateful parent found
the red marks on his shoulder made by the dog's mouth –
Bruce had had the intelligence not to hold on with his teeth.
What is even more amazing is that he had had the initiative to
lie on his side and not spreadeagle his legs, or he would also
have sunk in the mud.

Bruce, who originally came from Stratford-on-Avon, was
owned by Mrs G Gard, and was given to her for company by
her son who is in the police force. From the first the dog took

pleasure in the company of children living nearby and would accompany them to school. He frequently went to young Spencer's house to play with him and it was fortunate he did so on that particular day.

The dog's lifesaving ability delighted but did not really surprise his owner. The neighbours were gratified when Bruce was awarded a plaque by the RSPCA for his intelligent devotion.

Whilst Newfoundland dogs had for some time been assisting lifeguards on European beaches, few if any had been trained and used for lifesaving in Britain. In 1991 the first canine lifeguards gave demonstrations in Plymouth when specially trained Newfoundland dogs showed off their lifesaving skills. The dogs demonstrated a range of lifesaving skills, for instance swimming and towing a casualty. Just one more example of the way that dogs benefit humans.

The Baby Rabbit was a Brick

— ∞ — ∞ — ∞ — ∞ — ∞ —

A baby rabbit recently survived an incredibly horrific adventure in the mechanical jungle of the outside world.

Concrete blocks were being made at a quarry at Axminster, Devon, and one day, as the finished product was coming off the conveyor system, the workers were amazed to see movement in one of the blocks. First a crack and then 'pop', the head of a tiny rabbit emerged. He struggled out by his own efforts and was sitting on top of the block before anyone could even reach him to lend a hand.

He must have been scooped up with thirty tons of sand, thrown into the weighing hopper, and then carried by conveyor to an overhead mixer, where cement and water were added and the ingredients then swirled round and round at high speed. Next he must have passed into a machine where the wet cement was hammered into blocks by pressure of 100lb per square inch. The blocks, which measured 18in long × 9in high × 6in thick, were then ejected on to the floor where they were to remain for drying.

True, the rabbit was in a fearfully bedraggled state but he had survived. The men washed the cement from him, cleaned him up, dried him by an electric fire and then placed him near what must have been his point of entry. Away he hopped as if nothing had happened.

As the quarry manager said, it was a mystery how the little chap escaped unscathed for by rights he should have been suffocated, drowned, squashed or cut into pieces. What an escape story to tell his numerous brothers and sisters!

— ∞ — ∞ — ∞ — ∞ — ∞ —

Mongrel Saves Young Master

— ∞ — ∞ — ∞ — ∞ — ∞ —

IT was a bitter November day when Willie Fraser, aged seven, and his friend Tony went for a walk on the moorland near their home at Burnley, Lancashire. They were accompanied by Willie's constant companion, Lady, a mongrel dog who had recently attached herself to him. Probably they never intended to go far, but being boys they just wandered on. They were thinly clad; Willie wore only a jumper, vest, short trousers and rubber boots.

They started out in reasonable weather, but as often happens on the moors, conditions deteriorated rapidly. A gale-force wind blew up, bringing with it freezing sleet and a heavy downpour of rain. In such conditions the two boys became hopelessly lost, and as darkness began to fall Willie could go no farther. They had been wandering for four hours and he sank down exhausted against a moorland wall. His friend stumbled off to try and get help, whilst Lady remained with her young master.

Eventually Tony was found wandering near a farmstead where the farmer's wife took him in, gleaned some of his story and immediately raised the alarm. By then it was dark, but twenty policemen accompanied by two dogs moved into the area and began what they must have felt was a pretty hopeless task. The conditions were appalling, with the rough ground becoming a thick oozy mud. Suddenly Sabre, one of the police dogs, picked up a scent which led them to Willie, half a mile away. He was still lying against the same wall but was unconscious and over him, protecting him with her warm body, was Lady. They were some six miles from home!

The boy was rushed to hospital, where the doctor found that Willie's heart had stopped beating. They massaged it externally for half an hour and then gave the kiss of life. The heart began to beat again. The last word must come from Willie. 'It was very cold,' he said – surely the under-statement of the year – 'but Lady snuggled over me to keep me warm, and I don't remember anything after that.'

Lady, in her attachment to Willie, developed one endearing trait. Whenever Willie cried she went to him and licked his face until he stopped.

— ∞ — ∞ — ∞ — ∞ — ∞ —

From Kennel to Castle

— ∞ — ∞ — ∞ — ∞ — ∞ —

WHEN Kathy was a tiny puppy her large head and feet would have suggested to someone well used to dogs that she was likely to grow into a large animal. But the lorry driver who first purchased her as a companion was not that discerning; and as she grew and grew he was too fond of her to let her go until he lost his job – and then there was no alternative. He took her therefore to an animal sanctuary at Borough Green in Kent and left her, with the warning that no kennel or fence would hold her. Kathy was now fully grown, and a fully grown Pyrenean mountain dog at that!

People were prepared to take a chance over such a magnificent animal, but although eight different homes were found for her she stayed at none of them. The last owner was a Kent farmer and he returned Kathy after she had smashed the windows of the house to get out and then made her way to the M20 motorway, where she was nothing short of a menace.

Kathy in her short lifetime had already become famous. She had appeared on the children's television programme, *Blue Peter,* to highlight for children the problems of owning a large dog, special emphasis being placed on the size of her food bill. Her story, with pictures, had also made headlines in the press. This publicity saved the situation. The owner of the sanctuary received out of the blue an instruction which read:

'On no account have Kathy put to sleep. Put her on a flight from Heathrow addressed to: The Duchess of Alba, The Palace, Madrid.'

There was a feeling of immense relief, for it really had

looked as if the end of the road was looming for Kathy. Her food bill alone was a problem: weighing 56kg (115lb), with a 1m (36in) girth and standing 74cm (29in) high, she made short work of a basic daily allowance of one pint of milk, 1kg (2lb) cooked meat and 340gm (12oz) biscuit.

The Duchess of Alba, who confesses to a weakness for stray dogs had read about Kathy in a newspaper and immediately made arrangements for her to be sent to Madrid.

Kathy's new home is a 100-room castle, occupying a site of twenty-five acres. She has settled down happily with the family and the other dogs on the establishment.

It is a traditionally happy ending to the story of Kathy, the princess (albeit canine) and the fairy tale castle.

— ∞ — ∞ — ∞ — ∞ — ∞ —

Tara's Shocking Ordeal

— ∞ — ∞ — ∞ — ∞ — ∞ —

CRUELTY to animals comes in many forms and recently a beautiful eighteen-month-old alsatian was found chained to a tree stump on a miniature island in the river, which soon gets flooded in heavy rain. Obviously some sadist thought it would not be long before she was slowly drowned. She had been there about two days and in a pitiable condition. No wonder, for a series of marks round her chest showed she had been stabbed several times in the hollow of her chest. The dog, starved, in pain and terrified was in a shocking condition when found by two passers by out for a walk.

Mrs Sue Ford heard of the case and offered to take her and nurse her back to health. The dog was given food and was so ravenous that she grabbed at everything even the bowl.

Naturally it took weeks to gain her confidence. It was

found that she had bowel trouble, probably caused by being beaten and a skin complaint. Now Tara is the pride of the family which is made up of another alsatian, a King Charles and a Jack Russell and if she wants more company there is for good measure, a horse, three cats and a rabbit. All these animals accepted Tara right away as if they knew she had suffered.

Mrs Ford reports that the dog is now almost fully restored and adds that she would like to get her hands on the person responsible for just ten minutes. She is not alone in that thinking.

It would seem that this was another case of someone who instead of taking her to the vet and have her put down sought this way out. Why don't people, fed up with pets, take them to an Animal Centre or the vet and act like human beings instead of murderous outcasts?

Thank heaven there are such people as Mrs Ford and by their large heart and compassion go some way to counteract the viciousness and cruelty meted out to birds and animals which also have a place in this world.

— ∞ — ∞ — ∞ — ∞ — ∞ —

Only One Survived

— ∞ — ∞ — ∞ — ∞ — ∞ —

JACK Russells seem to make a habit of making headlines and the story of Sam, a six-year-old terrier, one of three, is another case of the wonderful courage and ability to sustain terror in awful conditions and still come up barking.

It happened at a Welsh village where again the three terriers were quick off the mark to chase a fox down a hole and they just disappeared. The RSPCA rescue team was called in and in no time at all a number of people anxious to help gathered.

It was found that the hole which was just a few inches wide led to a disused quarry. Among the helpers was an ex-miner who squeezed into the narrow hole and found it led to a tunnel of old mine workings. The entrance was widened and the miner was able to pick his way through for some 40ft where he found that one of the terriers had apparently followed its quarry. The terrier then went over the edge, to drop miraculously on to a ledge where sensibly he remained. The owner had maintained a constant vigil at the mouth of the cave – a period of waiting that went on for fifteen days.

Eventually the rescuer equipped with a rope noose found the terrier, but getting the rope round the frightened animal took over an hour as the dog kept pushing it away. Eventually it was successful and as he brought the dog out to daylight a cheer went up from those anxiously waiting.

Sadly the dog's two companions must have missed the ledge in their headlong rush of the chase and were never found.

Sam was caked in mud but none the worse for his fifteen day ordeal.

One has to admire the great courage of men who will take such risks to attempt such a rescue. As for the dog the mind boggles at what the poor little animal must have suffered in complete darkness for fifteen days.

It was one of the longest and most dangerous rescues ever mounted by the RSPCA rescue team and that they had ever undertaken.

One is left wondering whether the wily fox knew the underground passages and got away with it.

— ∞ — ∞ — ∞ — ∞ — ∞ —

Dogs' Ordeal in New Found Cave

— ∞ — ∞ — ∞ — ∞ — ∞ —

IT is quite amazing the way in which animals particularly cats and dogs will act in adversity.

Take two Jack Russell terriers who used to fight each other furiously. Then came the day when they found themselves imprisoned in an unknown cave for thirty hours. The horrific experience formed a common bond and they became bosom friends when they were rescued.

Their owner, Mr F Hutchings of Paignton, Devon, took them in his truck one day when he was to meet a friend at a builder's yard. As he opened the door to the truck the two dogs jumped out and were off at speed, presumably after a rat or rabbit, then they disappeared down a hole. The canines were father and son named Bonzo and Scamp, aged five and four and they always had seemed to lead a cat and dog life.

Anyhow they completely disappeared together down the hole behind the yard. All attempts to get them back failed. Tempting bowls of food and water were put at the mouth of the hole to no avail. Then it was found that they were trapped in a forgotten or lost underground cave and miraculously saved from falling into an underground lake for in their headlong chase they had landed on a narrow ledge.

Human rescuers enlarged the hole, squeezed into a narrow shaft and with drills worked to clear a ton of rubbish and hundredweights of rocks. After thirty hours of exhausting work they progressed far enough to hear the terriers whimpering. As they drew near to the ledge, the dogs growled but when their names were called they leapt straight into the arms of the rescuers.

Both were in a muddy mess, but otherwise unscathed. Returned safely to their owner they could not stop licking each other and they have been friends ever since.

— ∞ — ∞ — ∞ — ∞ — ∞ —

Jen's Common Sense

— ∞ — ∞ — ∞ — ∞ — ∞ —

THIS is the kind of story that leads us to equate the intelligence of a dog with that of a human.

Jen a five-and-a-half-year-old collie with the traditional colouring – black with a white blaze – was lost on Helvellyn, the second highest mountain in England (3,115ft). It was February, visibility was poor, there was also a lot of snow.

The intelligent canine, summed up the position, dug herself a hole in the snow under an overhanging rock and stayed there for six days and nights.

Jen and her master, Mr Murray, had climbed Helvellyn and were on their way down from the summit when poor visibility set in, which caused the dog to run over a heavily corniced edge and disappear.

The edge was so heavily corniced and unstable that Mr Murray crawled to the edge to look over but could not see her, just a steepish drop to where the rocks jut out about 30–40ft below. He hurried round to a safe way down and went up into the cove in the hope of finding Jen. He called and whistled but there was no sign of her and the visibility was by that time so bad with cloud descending that it was very difficult and dangerous.

Finally with darkness approaching the search had to be

abandoned for that day. Next morning John Murray
returned very early – and was on Helvellyn summit by eight
o'clock and searched as best he could across the cliff face,
climbing up and over the cornice in the hope of seeing her.

He deliberately sought as much publicity as possible via
Radio Cumbria, talking to everyone he met and telling them
the story. The Lake District Ranger Service was extremely
helpful and contacted all the local farmers and kept a wary
eye open for her when they were out and about. The search
was widened but always returned to Brown Cove

Nevertheless when Jen had been missing for six nights all
hope for her had been given up. Something however inspired
Mr Murray to have one more search and he returned to
Brown Cove about 500ft below the mountain peak.

On the way up he spoke to two climbers from Darlington
who intended to climb in Brown Cove. They set off ahead of
him and part way up the cliff roped up. Mr Murray was on
his own so going up had to be careful. He had left his ruck-
sack below and only had the ice-axe for aid. The cliff,
although steep and requiring care was by no means
dangerous except that the cornice above might be unstable.
The week, although snowy and frosty, had not been an
extremely cold one.

Suddenly one of the climbers called down, 'I can see your
dog.' Mr Murray called back, 'Is she alive?', to receive the
reply, 'Well, she's wagging her tail.' Asked if they could get
across to her, they replied 'Yes', so he made his way up to join
them. By the time Mr Murray got there, the climbers had tied
Jen to their rope and had given her a bun to eat.

She had dug herself a little snow hole below an overhanging rock and had obviously been there all week, and
from the marks around had only left the hole to relieve
herself. It was decided that the best thing to do was to take
her to the top which was only about 100–150ft above. Mr
Murray asked if he could tie on to the rope as he thought that
he might have to carry Jen but not a bit of it – she was able to
scamper up in their footprints until they reached the cornice

where he had to help her over the steep part. At the top of Helvellyn she wanted to play but her master tied her to a tape and having thanked the two climbers, took her down the safe way. She was thin but seemed well and the only damage the vet could find was that she had lost a front tooth.

She had obviously been eating snow as the front of her mouth was red and raw, although that may also have been when she lost the tooth, possibly by banging into a rock in her fall. The whole experience proves how very sensible some animals can be; she stayed where she fell, protected herself as best she could, then waited to be rescued. The only snag was as a friend said, 'She never barks when she is out with us,' so no doubt during her week she would have heard the Boss calling and whistling and just wagged her tail – thinking, 'Well I'm here why doesn't he come?'

Just a week before this happened to Jen, a highly valued search and rescue dog had been lost and was later seen from time to time circling the Fells. She was almost caught soon afterwards but a helicopter circling above frightened her off. She was eventually rescued. It was thought in the early stages that Jen would do the same, but Jen obviously thought it out and stayed put.

Incidentally to end this story I was amazed when interviewing Jen's owner, he talked of climbing Helvellyn much the same as most people would walk to the nearest post box.

— ∞ — ∞ — ∞ — ∞ — ∞ —

Jenny Gets Home Dragging a Gin Trap

— ∞ — ∞ — ∞ — ∞ — ∞ —

JENNY, a tabby, is one of two cats that live with the Wybrow family at Sandford near Crediton, Devon.

One day she disappeared and though the family of mother and five girls searched high and low she was not to be found.

Then thirty-six hours later some local lads found the poor cat in agony, dragging a vicious iron gin trap in which her right front paw had been caught. She was struggling to make her way home.

The boys got her home and she was rushed to the vet who decided there was no hope of saving the badly mangled leg and amputation was the only answer. The operation was very successful.

Her recovery rate was amazing and, on her return home after a few days, she was more affectionate to the family than ever. Aged three-and-a-half years, she also received solace from her daughter and companion cat.

Within a week or two Jenny was back on form, still managing to jump up and sit on top of the television on a cold night. The family did not welcome, but willingly paid, the vet's bill of £150.

RSPCA officials express their horror that people still set these vicious traps which have long been illegal and prosecute if ever they find the ghouls who set them. They warned that it might be a child's hand or foot next time.

— ∞ — ∞ — ∞ — ∞ — ∞ —

Sheep Rescued By Helicopter

— ∞ — ∞ — ∞ — ∞ — ∞ —

MUCH is being done to preserve the rare breeds of various animals and in 1991 Soay sheep, one of Britain's oldest breeds, were rounded up and lifted by helicopter from an island to the mainland.

It was a mammoth undertaking by over a hundred volunteers who transported them from Cardigan Island off the west coast of Wales, where they had only gulls for company, to the mainland where they have been found homes.

The flock of these hardy sheep were introduced to the forty acre island in 1944. They are native to Soay, part of the St Kilda group of islands fifty miles west of the Outer Hebrides.

The need to move them came about when tons of salt from sea spray were deposited on Cardigan Island during the storms of 1990. The dry summer prevented the grass recovering as the salt burnt patches, thus causing an acute shortage of grazing, forcing their keepers to save them from starvation.

During a day-long operation, the sheep were rounded up and driven along a funnel of netting and into a pen where each was weighed and measured.

With their feet trussed, the animals were then loaded into crates made of pallets and nets and airlifted fourteen at a time by RAF Sea King helicopter to a Dyfed farm where they were dipped before dispersal.

'The whole thing was very forbidding, but went much better than expected,' said Mr Mick Bains of the Dyfed

Wildlife Trust, one of the island's managers.

'We needed a lot of people to round up the sheep and then hold onto them, but although they are completely wild they were quite manageable.'

— ∞ — ∞ — ∞ — ∞ — ∞ —

Two of a Cat's Nine Lives

— ∞ — ∞ — ∞ — ∞ — ∞ —

THE inquisitiveness of cats is well known and often it gets them into strange places.

In this particular case Micky, a ginger tom, went missing for six days and his anxious owner heard that a neighbour believed the cat to be somewhere on her property, for she could hear him from time to time.

After a prolonged search, with permission the owner climbed scaffolding outside the house where intermittent cat cries had been heard. At first some slates were taken off the roof – some forty in all. Still Micky was not to be seen. Then it was realised that he must be trapped in the cavity of the wall.

Using a hammer and chisel several bricks were removed and there was the cat, wedged in the cavity.

He appeared unhurt, but was naturally shaken up and hungry after six days confinement.

Micky was formerly abandoned as a kitten in a busy street in Barnstaple, North Devon, but miraculously survived the traffic hazards. That was his first life written off.

His owner had another cat which also led a charmed life for he suffered a broken back after falling off a roof and was brought back to active life.

— ∞ — ∞ — ∞ — ∞ — ∞ —

The Terrier was Foxed

— ∞ — ∞ — ∞ — ∞ — ∞ —

MR Bailey of Cardiff was out with his terrier, Nipper, when he disappeared down a drain pipe which ran under a football field.

For two days the owner called and worried and at last hearing a bark, he called in the Fire Brigade. They dug two 4ft holes in the field and hearing the dog barking knew they were on the right track. They broke the drainage pipe and a fireman crawled through to find the terrier sitting opposite a fox. They had obviously met up in the pipe and neither would give way to allow one of them through for the pipe was only 18in in diameter. Nipper was very scared but otherwise well.

The firemen described the event as one of their more unusual rescues.

— ∞ — ∞ — ∞ — ∞ — ∞ —

In Love – He Fell Twenty Feet

— ∞ — ∞ — ∞ — ∞ — ∞ —

THE late Bernie Winters, the comedian and star of many shows, was a great dog lover and his St Bernard, Schnorbitz, became almost as well known for she frequently appeared on shows and pantomime with Bernie and was also a great collector for charities. She is probably the best known dog in Britain. But Schnorbitz was only one of several owned by the comedian. He had a fine German Shepherd, Ella, eleven years old, a miniature Yorkie, Putzi, two years old and two chihuahuas.

It seems however that Schnorbitz the 8st heavyweight is in every sense a great character.

In the summer of 1988 when her master was playing Babbacombe Theatre's *Crazy Gang Show* Schnorbitz fell in love. From her master's flat in Torquay she spotted a chihuahua 20ft below. She was enraptured and leaned too far out of the window. She fell, fracturing her shoulder. The result was that she was unable to go on the show. Cheeky the chihuahua who had gone to her heart took her place under the spotlights.

Schnorbitz, as a convalescent, was relegated to watching her boyfriend tread the boards from the wings.

Bernie's comment was, 'next time she tries jumping out of the window I'll make sure she wears a parachute'.

— ∞ — ∞ — ∞ — ∞ — ∞ —

Wandered on to the Tamar Bridge

— ∞ — ∞ — ∞ — ∞ — ∞ —

A schoolboy clambered up the 150ft high Tamar River suspension bridge, which links Devon and Cornwall, to rescue the two-year-old black-and-white family cat Tommy.

How the cat managed to get there and who first spotted him is a mystery, but when thirteen-year-old Jason Snell appeared on the scene, he did not hesitate.

He scrambled over a 50ft wall, then crawled up a 100ft angled girder and walked along the narrow walkway under the road bridge to reach the cat. The animal was frozen with fear but obviously recognised his rescuer, allowing him to tuck him inside his coat. Then he started to descend. Fortunately he found a piece of old rope which he calmly tied to a girder and lowered himself part way down.

He was applauded by the firemen and the crowd that had gathered.

The police ticked him off for the risk he had taken but Jason was unrepentant and said no one else could have rescued Tommy – he would have scratched them for he was so scared.

A fireman said they were deciding how to make the rescue and planned to lower a man through a manhole in the road.

The cat was reunited with Jason's ten-year-old brother with delight on both sides.

— ∞ — ∞ — ∞ — ∞ — ∞ —

Piglet Took to the High Road

— ∞ — ∞ — ∞ — ∞ — ∞ —

MOTORISTS on a main road at Axminster, Devon, were amused and surprised to see a very small pig trotting daintily along in the middle of the road.

He was quite tiny and but a week old when he was rescued by a farmer. No one knew where the piglet had come from so he was taken home to the friendly farmer and brought back to health by bottle feeding and keeping him warm in a box by the stove.

Then one day the small animal began to help himself from the cat's bowl.

Pinky the young collie in the house quickly made friends and the dog and pig became inseparable.

The only explanation was that he must have been in a trailer with his mother, felt the call of wanderlust and escaped for he had quite a number of scratches on him.

— ∞ — ∞ — ∞ — ∞ — ∞ —

Animal Actors

— ∞ — ∞ — ∞ — ∞ — ∞ —

A donkey which had a mind of its own is sixteen-year-old Simon who had a starring role in the Lloyd Webber musical *Joseph and the Amazing Technicolor Dreamcoat* at the Torquay Theatre.

During rehearsals he became acutely nervous when he got in front of the footlights and displayed his displeasure by nipping the actors and even kicking them to the accompaniment of a loud 'Hee-Haw'. He refused to move about the stage and worst of all used it as a convenience.

Faced with a perpetual headache, the producers cured his 'stage-nerves' by bringing into the wings his pal of five years, a horse called Copper. All was well.

So the show went on and Simon seemed pleased to show off his acting ability to his pal.

— ∞ — ∞ — ∞ — ∞ — ∞ —

Cat Bank Robber

— ∞ — ∞ — ∞ — ∞ — ∞ —

ANOTHER cat which went missing was an exotic pedigree Blue Point Balinese named Domingo. He had suddenly disappeared to the distress of his owner and was missing for some seven or eight weeks.

Staff at a Devon bank were investigating noises at the rear of their strong room. The strong room was opened and nothing was found so the cellars next to it were investigated and there found Domingo who was wearing a name tag.

The cat had apparently fallen 40ft down cliffs at the rear of the bank and found his way into the cellars. His owner lived just a few doors away from the bank.

There was of course a grand reunion.

The mystery as always in these cases is how an animal survives for such a long time in total darkness and without food or water.

— ∞ — ∞ — ∞ — ∞ — ∞ —

Digger – Australian Tough Guy

— ∞ — ∞ — ∞ — ∞ — ∞ —

TO adopt a stray in Australia and then, because it was unmanageable, pay $200 to send it 12,000 miles by air to England, as a VIP passenger, is quite something, even in the annals of the dog-loving fraternity. This was, however, what actually happened to Digger, a black cross spaniel, and he must be one of the luckiest, as well as one of the pluckiest, dogs alive. The full story is best told by the person concerned, Miss Val Lowe, who emigrated to Sydney from Margate, Kent:

' I first met up with Digger about three years ago when I was employed as a window-dresser at a store in the Sydney suburb of Compsie. At that time, the registration of dogs in this State had just been made compulsory and it was a common sight to see packs of abandoned dogs roaming the streets.

One little black dog in particular soon became a familiar sight hanging around the doors of the store. Obviously hungry, he still had a somewhat jaunty air about him which was immediately attractive. Being a soft touch, I suppose, I bought him an occasional tin of meat which was quickly dispatched. Suddenly after a few days he disappeared and I concluded that he had gone the way of most stray dogs, with the local dog-catchers!

However, some days later there he was again. This time in a pathetic condition, thin, one paw held in the air. Too much for me, I'm afraid! Against all practical reasoning, that night he was on his way home with me on the train.

A visit to the vet confirmed that he had an abscess in his paw, that he had 'rotten old teeth' and that he had had distemper as a pup. Not really a very good proposition as a dog! He was identified as a cross kelpie-spaniel. With this dingo ancestry the obvious name for him was Digger.

It soon became obvious that Digger loved all humans, and indoors he was a real pet. Once outside though, Jekyll became Hyde. Strangely, for all his previous wanderings, he had no road sense at all; a motor-cycle would produce a barking frenzy, and the sight of another dog would turn him into a tear-away thug. Dogs big or small, he would take them all on, with no qualms about tackling even an alsatian. His daily walks became a nightmare and a source of continual embarrassment. He became the terror of the harbourside park, which was nearest my flat. Other owners would promptly vanish round the nearest corner when Digger appeared. I have a vivid recollection of his seizing an unfortunate white poodle, who gradually changed in colour from white to grey to black as he was hauled through the mud, while its hysterical female owner broke her folding umbrella on Digger's head.

He could swim like a beaver, his favourite targets being the various ornamental pools in the vicinity. Once he nearly gave me heart failure by jumping into the harbour and swimming out until his head was a black dot in the distance, when he was whistled back by a kindly stranger.

As time went on it became obvious that keeping Digger cooped up in a flat was doing him no good at all. We were both becoming neurotic. What to do with him?

Hopefully, I advertised in the local paper. One reply only, for a guard dog, convinced me that this was not the solution. After a while the idea of sending him home to my parents took root. It was a big step but fortunately I had a friend who works for an international airline. He was able to make the whole idea feasible, even to the extent of arranging a concessionary fare.

So one morning a little later Digger left for England. I could not go to the airport but my friend reported that his last sight of Digger was of his jaunty flag of a tail still wagging as he was conveyed to the waiting 'V' jet.

Of course, it meant six months quarantine before he was finally turned over to my parents. Not that they were particularly keen to take him, even though they had just lost their pedigree golden retriever. However, gamely they agreed. So Digger arrived in Margate.'

Although the garden of the Lowe's home at Margate is a large one, it was not big enough for Digger. It just became a prison camp for him, with himself as the star escaper. The fence was built higher and higher, but still he managed to escape. On one occasion he was brought back in style from three miles in a motorised invalid carriage.

Then Miss Lowe's parents sent him to a correction school, but this had no effect whatsoever. Finally, in desperation, they sent him to be neutered, and that operation did have some effect, though no quite in the way intended – after a few weeks he put on so much weight that try as he might he could not jump over the fence.

Digger is now four-and-a-half-years-old and seems in some measure to have accepted his fate. He is still an affectionate pet indoors, but scowls at motor-cycles and other dogs through the front window, and often, by his far away look, gives the impression that he is running with the wild dingo pack, probably leading them far, far away.

Any boy who behaved like Digger would probably be given every benefit of the doubt. It would be pleaded that he had had a broken home, and that unless society did something for him he would finish up a delinquent. Who knows what happened to Digger in his puppyhood?

Miss Lowe and her parents have certainly given Digger the benefit of the doubt, and even if a delinquent, he has courage, quick wits and, at bedrock, lots of affection for those who have been so good to him.

— ∞ — ∞ — ∞ — ∞ — ∞ —

Fishermen Nearly Killed Her

— ∞ — ∞ — ∞ — ∞ — ∞ —

SYDNEY, a black-and-white collie, was tail wagging with a vengeance when he set out for his usual walk along the River Coly in Devon. Spotting a piece of bread he began to eat it and then began to suffer severe discomfort.

His owner hurried to his aid and was shocked to find a length of fishing line hanging from his mouth. He had swallowed some hooks attached to the line which were obviously hidden in the bread. He was hurried to the vets and an x-ray revealed two hooks between the dog's throat and stomach. They operated and battled for three hours, having to remove two ribs to get at them.

The owner, Mrs J Sibley, was then told that further operations to get at the hooks were inadvisable for fear of risking the dog's life, so they remained inside him.

Residents of the small town of Colyton and nearby Seaton were touched by the case and set out to raise more than £100 towards the vet's bill.

He was one of the lucky ones. How many animals and birds such as swans and ducks die in agony because of the thoughtlessness and carelessness of anglers.

Some of the fund raisers walk the river daily and say they often retrieve pieces of line.

The RSPCA are constantly reminding anglers to clear up properly after them.

On this occasion, however, it was thought that the tackle was the type commonly used by poachers to trap ducks.

There was however a happy ending to this episode for in desperation the owner of the dog turned to alternative medicine which miraculously seems to have worked.

Now Sydney is back for his walks and we hope has learned not to pick up scraps.

— ∞ — ∞ — ∞ — ∞ — ∞ —

Bloodhound's Victory Roll

— ∞ — ∞ — ∞ — ∞ — ∞ —

NO collection of 'Rescued and Rescuers' stories would be complete without some reference to the bloodhound, Capella Podlea, owned by Dr and Mrs Hull, of Coleman's Hatch, Sussex. On at least two occasions Dumpy, as she is affectionately known, has been successful in tracing another missing dog.

The first was when she tracked a sealyham terrier to a badger's sett. Capella literally ran the terrier to earth some 5ft underground. When she came to the hole, she put her ear to it listening, it seemed, for the sound of breathing. Then, satisfied, she did what was tantamount to a victory roll, by rolling over on her back as is the way with bloodhounds when they run their quarry to earth. It took several men some hours to get the terrier out, but finally he was rescued none the worse for his adventure.

The next time Capella was called upon was when Rajah, a long-haired chihuahua, the pet of fourteen-year-old Christopher Fulford-Brown of Sussex, disappeared through the hedge of his garden. Many hours were spent searching for him, but in vain. As a last resort, someone suggested seeking the services of the bloodhound which had been in the news, and in due course Capella was brought to the scene. Her owners felt that, after such a long period, the scent might be too faint; nevertheless, she was taken to Rajah's bed where she sniffed to pick up the scent. Then the party set off – and what a trail it proved to be. Capella led them on a twelve-mile trek across fields, through woods, under barbed wire and over boggy land. Overcoming her instinctive terror of traffic, she took her posse across four main roads, till at last, after nearly three-and-a-half hours, the chihuahua was found. People had seen the little dog running wildly around and had, in fact, telephoned the police, but they had mistakenly described him as a Yorkshire terrier.

So this magnificent tracker earned her second RSPCA plaque, for services very well rendered. She was the only dog ever to win this highest award twice.

Capella is descended from a bitch in the Lake District, where bloodhounds are frequently used to track humans. The Scottish police also use them, though other police forces in the United Kingdom generally choose alsatians. Bloodhounds were extremely popular in Britain before the war, but their numbers were drastically reduced to five, due to the difficulty of feeding them under wartime conditions. It is estimated that there are now about 1,000 in the British Isles. They have big appetites and Capella ate some 3lb of meat every day in addition to biscuits and milk.

— ∞ — ∞ — ∞ — ∞ — ∞ —

The Perfect Mimic

— ∞ — ∞ — ∞ — ∞ — ∞ —

IT would seem that nothing is safe in this world for a thief stole a grey African parrot worth, apart from the sentimental value, probably £2,000.

It belonged to a Mr & Mrs Greenwood of New Ollerton, Nottingham.

Two years old, the family bought him from a pet shop and he fast became a real family pet.

There was only one drawback however. Mickey was a perfect mimic but some of his language could be embarrassing if for instance the local vicar called. The previous owner was undoubtedly a football fan and taught him to say, 'Here we go, here we go'.

The mind boggles as to how he picked up 'Show us your knickers'. His wolf whistle was perfection as was his rendering of part of 'Colonel Bogey'. Many other pieces came out which are unrepeatable.

Soon after the theft the owners saw a likeness in a seedy pet shop but it was quite impossible to prove it was Mickey.

Perhaps if the bird uses some of the words not used in public, he may eventually find his way back to the owners who offered a £1,000 reward.

— ∞ — ∞ — ∞ — ∞ — ∞ —

Swan is Rescued

— ∞ — ∞ — ∞ — ∞ — ∞ —

THE pollution of streams and rivers has become a terrible menace to all wildlife and it is something man can have little cause to be proud of.

A family of swans made a beautiful flotilla on the River Exe, when mother, father and seven little cygnets seen in convoy gave immense pleasure to all who saw them. Then, one day, tragedy struck when the mother of the family was seen in difficulties. She had paddled through an oil slick and her beautiful white feathers became hopelessly clogged.

Bystanders rescued the whole family, and called in an Inspector of the RSPCA who sent them to their Wildlife Field Unit at Taunton, Somerset. There it was found that only the mother of the brood was affected. It took two people some four hours to clean her and fortunately the little ones were unharmed. The family were later returned to the river and sailed off with their usual majestic pose.

Human interest, patience and skill had won the day.

— ∞ — ∞ — ∞ — ∞ — ∞ —

Dog Leads Searchers to Mistress

— ∞ — ∞ — ∞ — ∞ — ∞ —

PENNY is a sixteen-year-old mongrel and while she may be slowing up she proved to very good effect that she was in good voice.

Owned by Mrs S Hockings who lives near the Devon beauty spot, Woodbury Castle, they set off rather late on a winter afternoon for their daily walk. There are numerous paths and this time they took one which led to a dense plantation. Darkness descended unusually early and quickly Mrs Hocking, who is elderly, soon got lost.

She shouted for help until she was hoarse. By then it was totally dark and the dog sensed something was wrong.

Meanwhile the lady's husband had become worried about his wife's long absence and alerted the police who sent up their helicopter, using a thermal image camera, but this proved ineffective due to the trees and thick undergrowth of the area. The police then enlisted the help of the Royal Marines from a nearby depot and Mr Trevor Bartlett, Nature

Reserve Warden for the area, and co-ordinated a ground search.

More than four hours passed since she had set out and Mrs Hockings almost gave up hope, and by then she was unable to continue calling for help.

The dog obviously sensed that something was wrong and wandered off where quite possibly his acute hearing heard the searchers. So he began to bark and quite shortly Mr Hockings heard and recognised the bark. The dog led the rescuers to the spot.

It was 8.30pm bitterly cold and totally dark. Her ordeal had lasted more than four hours.

Mrs Hockings knows the area fairly well and said she would have been able to find her way out but for the almost complete darkness.

Fortunately she was wearing a warm hooded coat and boots so did not suffer unduly from the bitter cold and frightening ordeal.

If other walkers risk getting lost and have no wise old dog, she advises them to carry a whistle, an idea corroborated by Trevor Bartlett.

Penny received a Mars Bar when they were safely home.

Sheba the Collie

THIS is the tale of a young dog which had a happy ending. It concerns Sheba who was owned by a Greek family living in north London. When they found that Sheba was about to give birth to pups, the family hurried round to the RSPCA and dumped her. She was nine months old.

In due course she produced some lovely puppies for which homes were quickly found. Meanwhile this fine cross-bred collie, dark brown and white with a beautiful head, was in quick succession taken from her home and then from her pups.

A young couple decided to obtain a dog and went to the RSPCA to find one. Such visits are always painful to animal lovers. The barking that goes on when hope must spring in them that they may be the 'chosen' one is invariably evident.

There were such a lot to chose from but eventually the choice fell on Sheba who was by then eighteen months old. She had that lovely appealing look and seemed intelligent.

She was taken to her new home and whilst she had obviously been cared for her coat was dull, but her tail wagging mechanism was in perfect order though her muzzle was raw from looking through the bars. Then the fun began.

The dog had obviously had some training and had obviously not been allowed upstairs. She was perfectly house trained but simple commands – to sit or stay – did not register, which was rather a puzzle. It was some time before the new owners realised that she had been semi-trained in Greek. Sheba knew no English, the couple knew no Greek. So it was a fresh start and the dog soon became bi-lingual.

The next hurdle came when she was taken out and after a while let off the lead. She was dumbfounded, just couldn't believe it. To actually run on that green stuff known as grass was beyond her comprehension. Other dogs were about and she just loved making friends and racing around, though getting her back proved a bit of a problem.

One day an unknown in the form of a squirrel popped up on a country walk. Sheba was off excited as could be but she returned in minutes. She failed to catch the squirrel but instead had a nasty gash in her leg where she had caught in in barbed wire. She proved a stoic however and healed quickly. One more lesson learned in this great new world of hers.

The day came when she was taken to the seaside. She trod delicately on the sand, at first looking bewildered then delighted – think of all this sand just for her to play on. The approach to the waves fascinated her, but she took care not to get her feet wet.

But that is all in the past now she has had a minor brush with her first cat. She sits up in the car and watches the world go by. Her coat shines and she just adores her new owners – a feeling which is mutual. She is proving highly intelligent and a quick learner.

Sheba was taken to a house where there was a fine black cat which was used to dogs, and the feline just gazed at the dog but this again was a part of Sheba's new world. She stood off looking amazed then unfortunately barked. It was only a meek bark, but who knows in dog language it might have been surprise, a welcome or maybe she expected a bark in return. But the cat sprang into action, spitting, the hair on her back stood up and her claws came out. Sheba considered discretion the better part of valour and retreated. In two days cat and dog nonchalantly ignored each other and on a longer acquaintance would have been pals.

Sheba is a beautiful dog and gives joy to her owners. It is sad to reflect that all over the country there are kennels where unwanted dogs have just been dumped. Sadly dogs are left on motorways, even tied up and left in an empty house when their owners have moved.

— ∞ — ∞ — ∞ — ∞ — ∞ —

Emma Survived the Hazards

— ∞ — ∞ — ∞ — ∞ — ∞ —

MOST cat owners know that cats know how to entwine themselves into the owner's heart. They also so often take exception to what they consider an affront to their dignity and go into a huff.

Such a case was Emma, a Chinchilla with a most unusual colouring of grey and white referred to as shaded silver. She was given to her owners, Mr and Mrs E. Galloway of Hordle, on the edge of the New Forest, when she was six weeks old and quickly established herself as a determined and very independent member of the household. Even after the kitten stage for a period she would ignore all food unless spoon fed.

She grew up into a beautiful animal and roamed what she considered was her own territory – her garden and those of the two houses either side. Not for her the terrors of busy roads, farm dogs, foxes etc.

Then Mr and Mrs Galloway decided to take a five week holiday in Australia. Emma who was now nine years old was taken to board at the local cattery.

After five days Emma, obviously disillusioned with being parted from her home, felt enough was enough and on the fifth night made her escape by biting through the wire of the wire roofing above the run which was 7ft above her. She must have crossed a main road which in itself was remarkable, for she was terrified of traffic, and then completely disappeared.

In due course her owners returned and were naturally devastated. They searched high and low, night and day, until they say people thought they were insane. They were joined by two ladies, Janette Lawrence and Yvonne Frankland, of the Cat & Kitten Rescue Service of Lymington, nearby, and almost giving up hope, offered a £1,000 reward. Within twenty-four hours of the advertisement appearing in the local paper, there was a telephone call saying that a cat answering to Emma's description was seen in a garden several times over a period of three weeks, but had been quite unapproachable. Mrs Galloway went to the address and called the cat and after a while heard Emma's answering call and soon she appeared. When an attempt was made to pick her up, with a bound she was off with only a handful of fur remaining to show her appearance had not been fantasy.

Then a trap was laid by the two ladies from the Cat

Services with chicken as bait and at midnight a message came through that the cat was caught. The trap was taken home and sure enough Emma stepped out. The owners were very obviously delighted, but so too was Emma who did not stop purring for twenty-four hours. She had been running wild for over seven weeks. Her coat was in perfect condition but she started to attack a back paw in a frenzied manner.

The vet was of the opinion that a sliver of grass had worked its way into the paw and it was necessary to open the foot up to the joint. The surgery was successful and the grass and seed were removed. It was the vet's opinion that she had been found in time. In another twenty-four hours she would have bitten her paw off with the pain and irritation.

It would need a Sherlock Holmes of the animal world to work out how this home loving and obviously spoiled cat managed to exist in the world outside and the perils that went with it. She must have met up with some real hazards. Where did she get food? She showed no sign of hunger and her coat was in good condition. We shall never know, but it does show that we generally underrate the high intelligence of these four-footed pets.

The £1,000 reward was offered to the two ladies of the Cat and Kitten Rescue Service of Lymington but they refused to make financial gain from the sadness and loss of others. So Emma's owners have decided to support them in their work as and when it is possible in the future. The lady who made the telephone call was given £75 for her trouble.

Incidentally Emma now has a companion – a kitten named Tara.

— ∞ — ∞ — ∞ — ∞ — ∞ —

Some Nest Egg

— ∞ — ∞ — ∞ — ∞ — ∞ —

IT is not often that a humble cockerel turns to hunting for treasure. It may well have been the first time for Bertie, but he certainly uncovered a crock of gold.

It happened at Mountfitchet Castle at Stanstead, Essex, owned by a businessman, Mr A Goldsmith.

The Norman castle, a tourist spot, is built on the site of earlier fortifications, and domestic animals some of them rare breeds occupy an enclosure.

Miss Dryden was idly watching the birds when she noticed Bertie, a Buff Orpington cockerel, head down scratching frantically at an old rabbit warren. As she watched she noticed what looked like dirty old half-pennies being cast out. Closer inspection revealed that they were Roman coins. She called the owner and together they got down on hands and knees, digging excitedly with their hands. Miss Dryden said it was a great thrill as the pile grew.

There was altogether a hoard of what proved to be first century Roman coins provisionally worth between £3 and £8 each.

When the treasure has been examined, it will be decided whether a prima facie case has been made for an inquest. If declared treasure trove, the value will be shared between Mr Goldsmith and Miss Dryden.

The hoard was put on show at the castle and without doubt there is an extra strut as Bertie walks about searching for other rabbit warrens.

— ∞ — ∞ — ∞ — ∞ — ∞ —

A Cliff Rescue

— ∞ — ∞ — ∞ — ∞ — ∞ —

BEN is a guide dog to his blind owner Mr C. Palmer who with his wife and daughter went on holiday to Cornwall. While walking the cliffs, the dog was let off his harness so that he could exercise freely.

Naturally Ben enjoyed his new found freedom and he ran around enjoying himself – then he disappeared. What exactly happened is not known, perhaps he discovered a rough path down to the shore but he could not be seen.

Eventually he was found to have slipped on loose shale and slithered down to rest on a ledge some 12ft above the sea. What happened afterwards is pure conjecture for he went into the water and swam to a small cove and an auxiliary coastguard cliff team was called to the scene.

It was then that a Wessex Search and Rescue helicopter passing on a training flight spotted the dog and decided to help. An aircrew man went down on a line but Ben, obviously frightened, ran off. He was eventually caught, wrapped in a blanket and successfully lifted off and taken to the cliff top where there was a joyful reunion with his master.

ANIMAL FRIENDSHIPS

— ∞ — ∞ — ∞ — ∞ — ∞ —

— ∞ — ∞ — ∞ — ∞ — ∞ —

Three Faithful Collies

— ∞ — ∞ — ∞ — ∞ — ∞ —

THE controversy over the intelligence of animals will perhaps never be resolved. There are those who are certain that animals have only instinct; others are convinced of their capacity for reasoning. Whatever the answer, animals often leave us amazed at their behaviour in difficult or dangerous circumstances.

One such example must surely be that of the three sheep-dogs belonging to a shepherd living near Callander in the Trossachs district of Scotland. The shepherd left the farm, accompanied by his three dogs, at 9am on a winter's morning to see to the 1,200 sheep in his care, some of which were missing beyond the great hills which form a backcloth to the little town. But the weather deteriorated badly and he failed to return. He had been missing eleven hours when the alarm was raised by the arrival back at the farm of one of his collies. The twin hazards of heavy snowfall and thick fog made it impossible to start a search that night, but next morning an RAF mountain rescue team, police foresters, shepherds, gamekeepers and other volunteers, aided by a helicopter, mounted a search.

The weather was still atrocious and the helicopter had to be withdrawn, but those on foot struggled on. Eventually one of the police constables, making slow progress through the snow and mist, was halted by a deep growl. He found the two collies standing guard over the body of their master. All night they had waited in those awful conditions, and now they were ready to attack the constable as he approached. It appeared that soft snow on the hills had yielded beneath the shepherd's weight and he had fallen 500ft to his death. The people of the Trossachs mourned the loss of one whom they held in great affection and esteem.

One wonders what sort of reasoning went on in the minds of those dogs. Humans in the same situation would have considered which could best make the return journey and raise the alarm. Perhaps they would have tossed a coin for it. In the same way, two of the animals elected to stay on guard, while the other went for help.

— ∞ — ∞ — ∞ — ∞ — ∞ —

Playmates Unlimited

— ∞ — ∞ — ∞ — ∞ — ∞ —

FOR years past in Harrogate, Yorkshire, Jack, a taxi-driver's dog, had amused many and pestered some by his trick of getting someone to play with him.

Jack accompanies his master to work every day and makes his base at the drivers' shelter at the taxi rank on the edge of the Stray, an open space. When his master goes off with his first fare, Jack has his morning snooze and then wakes up wanting his exercise. The fact that there is no other dog to play with does not worry him one bit; he goes to the nearest public bench, the type that seats about six people, and nudges in the back the first person that takes his fancy. Having thus gained attention, he trots round to the front and drops his ball at his chosen victim's feet. Usually the person responds, and that is his great mistake, for the game goes on and on and on. No rest is allowed and the human's only hope of relief is to walk away.

Jack then remains pensive for a while. One can almost feel him weighing up the possibilities of the people that are left.

However, his selection made, by some formula known only to himself, he repeats his routine. First a nudge in the back, then the presentation of the ball, and off the game goes once more.

Sometimes the bench is empty; but Jack knows the answer to that one. Far too wise to sit too near, he retires to the foot of a tall tree within sight of the seats, and, pretending to sleep, keeps perpetual vigilance. Strange to say, he does not jump forward to the first person who sits down. It seems he or she has to pass his personal test, and that once the person with the necessary qualifications pauses to rest, Jack goes over to make acquaintance. Rarely does he make a bad choice, and almost always his chosen playmate responds.

Jack is as adamant about his territorial rights as he is about making people play. Four public paths cross his area, and when a dog running free comes near, Jack puts on an act of ferocious barking. If, on the other hand, the trespassing dog is on a lead, he is magnificently ignored.

Jack became an institution in that part of Harrogate and a continual source of interest to people nearby – particularly those watching from a safe distance!

— ∞ — ∞ — ∞ — ∞ — ∞ —

A Touching Friendship

— ∞ — ∞ — ∞ — ∞ — ∞ —

ONE of the most remarkable stories is that of the beginning, duration and ending of the strange and unusual friendship between a hen and a cat, at the home of Mrs Collier in the village of North Cadbury in Somerset.

There were two cats on the establishment. One had been a permanent member of the household for a long time. The other was a stray that just turned up. He was not accepted by the other cat and at first they quarrelled continually; but then, as animals so often do, they arrived at a compromise acceptable to both. The household pet reigned indoors, and the stray took up his vantage point on a window sill and slept in the conservatory, so that they rarely met.

This was the situation when one fine summer afternoon a hen arrived, and settled down on the window sill that the stray had claimed as his domain, helping herself to a drink of milk from his bowl. She was a fine glossy Rhode Island Red, well fed and in good condition. Later in the afternoon the tom cat returned and jumped up to his window sill. Strange to say, even at this first meeting the cat evinced no surprise, nor indeed did he seem in the least bit curious, unusual at any time for a cat.

Inquiries were made in the district, but no one seemed to have lost a hen, so she stayed on with the cat. The pair became inseparable companions, sharing the window sill during the day and sleeping quarters in the conservatory at night. The cat slept on a bed of hay, the hen perched on a shelf above, and they ate together from the same bowl each giving way to the other in turn. Three weeks later the hen showed her appreciation by laying a large brown egg. This became a daily event and she always laid the egg in the same place.

So this strange pair settled into a pattern which never changed. Every day when the cat was groomed, the hen would fuss around until she too was brushed. That also became a daily routine. Meanwhile the other cat ignored them both. Two years passed in this tranquil fashion, until one day the cat was hit by a passing car, a fact that was only discovered when Mrs Collier went to give the pair their breakfast. Only the hen was there and eventually the cat was found lying on his bed of hay badly hurt. He was conscious and managed to lap up some cream but he could not stand and his head was injured. The vet arrived but could do nothing except put him out of his misery. The hen stood by, watching every move intently, though she was taken out when the cat was put down. That evening the hen was in her usual place for a meal which she had before going off into the conservatory for the night as usual. It was the last anybody saw of her!

Naturally, the strange association of the two was known to the people in the village, and with their help a thorough search was made in fields, woods and gardens over a wide area, but the hen was never seen again and no report of anyone having seen her ever came to hand.

Who knows, as Mrs Collier says, whether the hen is wandering, searching for the cat who shared her life so closely.

— ∞ — ∞ — ∞ — ∞ — ∞ —

Six Cats and a Mouse

— ∞ — ∞ — ∞ — ∞ — ∞ —

I am indebted to Miss Dorcie Sykes who lives at Newlyn, Cornwall, for the following true story.

'On looking through my window one day, I was surprised to see a half-circle of six cats sitting round a door in the street below my window. Whatever are they doing? I thought. They seem to be holding a meeting.

There was Sylvester a grey cat and Pander a black-and-white cat, both neighbour's cats, and my large black cat Sooty with a withered ear, an old warrior scarred by many fights, Daisy my little tabby cat and big Titch a very fine tabby cat, and another neighbour's cat called Jinger.

I hurried downstairs out through the back down into the street, I stood a little distance behind the group and watched, for they were oblivious to my presence so intent were they on watching. All were taut with eyes never wavering from the door to the street.

Suddenly from under the door appeared a small head, a little mouse's head, two bright little eyes and little sharp nose. It disappeared in and out several times. Poor mouse! It was in trouble. I clapped my hands and made several loud shoo's. The three neighbour's cats ran off in different directions but my cats had to be put inside through the back door, in fact they were quite annoyed.

I waited some distance away from the door; the tiny head appeared again several times and really made quite sure the coast was clear. Mousy came out, body flattened like a door mat to get through under the door. And off down the street, me in silent pursuit; it turned into an alleyway and down over some steps, across a courtyard and into a stone wall of a garden, safely back home. I don't think it would ever venture up the street again and who could blame it?'

— ∞ — ∞ — ∞ — ∞ — ∞ —

Henry, Quintin and the Fox

— ∞ — ∞ — ∞ — ∞ — ∞ —

MISS M Price of Bexhill, on the Sussex coast, had a surprise when she found that the bread and milk she had put out for a pair of hedgehogs was being shared by a friendly fox. Bexhill, with a population of around 35,000, can scarcely be considered rural, yet Miss Price is continually being amazed at the way wild creatures call in on her.

The two hedgehogs were old friends. They dropped by one evening, were fed and thereafter made a nightly call for six months or more. Christened Henry and Quintin, each had distinct personalities and characteristics. Henry was a mild little fellow, but his friend could, if need be, become quite belligerent. One night while the two of them were enjoying the meal, a young fox sauntered up. He made no effort to hurt the hedgehogs and quickly joined in the meal, sharing the same bowl. It must have been superlatively good bread and milk, for he too began to make a nightly call. Just occasionally he so far neglected his manners as to try and exclude his fellow diners, but the more belligerent of the two promptly backed into him, his spine meeting the fox's nose, and emitted an odd hissing noise at the same time. Thereafter the fox took the hint and behaved himself.

With the approach of winter the hedgehogs settled into the compost heap for their long sleep but the fox continued to come, and not without good reason, for, since the departure of the hedgehogs, his nightly repast consisted of breast of mutton.

One evening, looking out from her window, Miss Price was somewhat surprised to see a piece of lamb moving across the garden apparently under its own power. When she investigated, she found that it was in fact being dragged along by a tiny soft-bristled hedgehog. At that very moment the fox appeared. Realising that this was his own supper being whisked away, he grabbed the meat, shook off the hedgehog and calmly proceeded to eat his meal. Whether he would have shaken Quintin off with the same ease is a matter for conjecture.

When the seasons turned full circle, the original trio became a foursome, for one night the fox arrived with a beautiful, fluffy, greedy little cub which proceeded to bolt down all the bread and milk put down for the hedgehogs. But disregarding the bad manners of the newcomer the hedgehogs and fox continued to pay their nightly call, all three once more eating amicably together.

— ∞ — ∞ — ∞ — ∞ — ∞ —

Strange Playmates

— ∞ — ∞ — ∞ — ∞ — ∞ —

HILDA is a hamster who has a three-storey house of her own, but lives with five nurses in East London. She is a playful little thing who never seems bored. She feeds on the ground floor of her dwelling, plays on the first floor and, believe it or not, runs upstairs to bed on the top floor.

When she first took up residence, the girls in the house could never understand how it was that she had escaped in their absence and was found running round the room. It took weeks before it was discovered that when they purchased her miniature home they had omitted to clip the roof down. Hilda soon discovered the omission and when the girls came off duty very tired they were not amused at having to run round trying to capture Hilda – but it was a game in which she revelled.

This small attractive animal was often let out to play with a ball which she also enjoyed immensely. When she had been in residence about a year, another pet was introduced to the house, a six-week-old kitten, and there was a fear that if Hilda escaped again the kitten's claws would finish her off.

Then came the day when, with bated breath, the girls let Hilda out for a formal introduction to the kitten. To everyone's surprise they started to play. Hilda fetched her ball and in minutes they were pushing it to and fro, thoroughly enjoying themselves and it soon became a daily routine.

What is more, Jessica, the kitten, waits patiently every evening with her nose, not claws, at the hamster's cage, knowing that when the girls return she will be let out so that their daily ball game will take place.

— ∞ — ∞ — ∞ — ∞ — ∞ —

Goat Feeds Foal

— ∞ — ∞ — ∞ — ∞ — ∞ —

DOMESTIC animals of every kind if left to their own devices seem to be able to strike up the most unlikely friendships.

The classic case in my experience was the story of the cat and the hen told earlier on p105.

Another unlikely couple were a two-day-old foal and a nanny goat which came about in 1991 on a Devon farm.

The foal was born and regrettably the mother had to be put down due to a leg injury. Attempts were made to find a surrogate mother but none were immediately available. It was then that Mrs Mingo, the farmer, had a brain wave and borrowed a nanny goat from a neighbour, for cow's milk is too high in fat whereas goat's milk is much more easily digestible.

It was an instant success. The goat had to be raised by standing on a bale of straw and the young foal went to work.

It became a regular thing. Some supplementary food was provided as the colt grew but the goat provided the basic.

The friendship continued between the two animals until the colt had to be brought into the paddock, a period of some three months.

— ∞ — ∞ — ∞ — ∞ — ∞ —

The Blind Puppy

— ∞ — ∞ — ∞ — ∞ — ∞ —

FRIENDSHIPS between animals, particularly in giving help to a creature less fortunate than themselves, often occur and an amazing example of this occurred when two eight-week-old labrador collie puppies were brought into an Animal Rescue Centre. Both were very beautiful, one black and one brown, but it was soon discovered that the brown one seemed to have no sense of direction and after watching for a day or two it was found that the little chap, who incidentally had lovely eyes, was totally blind.

His brother and companion, the black one, also had noticed something was wrong and took to nudging him gently towards his food bowl at feeding time. The same at bedtime, he was nudged to his bed. When they got into the run they soon began to frolic and play as puppies do and the brown one entered in to the games with zest.

No one coming in to see them wrestling or playing tug of war with a lead would ever have noticed that one had no sight. Having found one end of a lead he would wrestle with great energy.

Nevertheless, nature has a way of compensating and making adjustment and the little chap had a remarkably good ear and would head unerringly to the spot where a voice came from, and once he had been around seemed to be able to find his way to any given spot again.

This story made television and newspaper news and stated that a home was wanted for both puppies to be kept together. The result was amazing for some hundreds offered to give them a home. The story in the international press attracted many offers.

The kennels which dealt with this difficult problem so sympathetically were at Castleford, situated in a hamlet near Newton Abbot, Devon. Run by Mr and Mrs Spier who have been in business many years, they have had a great many terrible cases of cruelty brought to them including one of a beautiful spaniel which had been all but kicked to death. Another well remembered case was that of a fine bloodhound which was brought to them when found wandering in the vicinity. They took the dog in and eventually found it had left home in Bristol and wandered down to East Devon. It had been on the road a long time.

Sad to say the little brown puppy died from a brain injury which had caused his loss of sight the day before the pups were due to be picked up by a couple from Truro. They were so saddened that they refused the survivor. He was quickly taken up by a couple, Mr and Mrs Boughey, whose last dog Sailor died after a good life of fourteen-and-a-half years and this new one was so much like him in colouring. He was named Skipper and quickly settled into his new home. He passed his days like all puppies – playing, chewing and sleeping and in a matter of days became one of the family. Sad to say he soon fell ill and died.

— ∞ — ∞ — ∞ — ∞ — ∞ —

Horse Becomes a Guide Dog

— ∞ — ∞ — ∞ — ∞ — ∞ —

AT a Pony Rescue Centre at Enmore, near Bridgwater, Somerset, is a home for horses and ponies rescued from ill treatment and slaughter houses.

One resident was a long term and very bad tempered

horse, Moonflower, who had gained a fearsome reputation for bullying other horses. There must have been hundreds of them who had been bitten and kicked, until they knew their place.

Then came April who was blind, a very special case for she needed someone to guide her around. Moonflower seemed to realise that the new arrival needed help, for from the outset she went straight to her and nuzzled her all over. From then on the two horses became inseparable, and to all intents and purposes April had obtained a guide dog. It was absolutely uncanny.

April was bought by Annabele Walker, the Enmore Centre owner, for £300 when she was four weeks away from giving birth, and on the verge of being sold to the slaughter house. The foal was stillborn.

— ∞ — ∞ — ∞ — ∞ — ∞ —

A Bantam and Three Dogs

— ∞ — ∞ — ∞ — ∞ — ∞ —

EVERY so often we hear of strange friendships which occur between birds and animals which sometimes seem to bring about an identity crisis.

This was so with Peanuts a rare Polish bantam and three dogs. The bird was one of a pair purchased by Lady Molesworth who obtained the bantams to join her peacocks and Guinea fowl already on show at her lovely house Pencarrow, near Bodmin, Cornwall.

It did not, however, work out that way. The first bantam Popcorn ran foul of the peacocks and died, but Peanuts was made of stronger stuff and whilst her hate of peacocks was mutual she had the good sense to stay close to the house.

This led to the bird taking charge of the three dogs. Her food bowl is put down with those of the dogs.

She would take a look at her own bowl, just treat it as an hors d'oeuvre and then quickly move over to the bowls of the three dogs, a retriever and two spaniels, push them aside and taking her time, pick all she wanted. The dogs meanwhile stand by drooling but taking no action. Satisfied at last, Peanuts then returns to her own bowl.

When the house is open to the public Peanuts takes up station on the back of a chair in the hall and eyes the visitors, for all the world like a security guard.

So she remains until ten minutes to five and she times it to the minute. She then leaves her post and reminds her mistress that the house closes at 5pm.

In the evening she takes up her self-appointed position on the back of Lady Molesworth's chair and seems to watch the television, (or perhaps enjoys being one of the family).

Apart from anything else it would seem that bantams, like dogs, have their own inbuilt clock which tells them the time.

— ∞ — ∞ — ∞ — ∞ — ∞ —

Dillys the Duck and Playmate

— ∞ — ∞ — ∞ — ∞ — ∞ —

ANIMALS make queer friendships and one of the strangest is that between Dillys, one of the largest and most handsome ducks possible to find, and Gemma a lively collie cross. Beautifully marked she appears to be nine-tenths border collie.

The duck was incubated and when hatched came to live in

a family home. Soon after she was able to waddle around, the dog who had been with the family since a puppy, some six years, became fascinated and then cautiously crept nearer to sniff. There was no resentment for the newcomer. Obviously what she smelt, she liked, and this amazing friendship developed. The duck (whether a drake or not) like Topsy grew and grew until she is now even bigger than a large goose, with a superb wing spread.

Both bird and dog grew up on the basis of anything you can do, I can do better. If Gemma leapt the wall and wire netting of the enclosure the bird would do the same, even if she did have to rest on the wall before the next stage over the wire. She seemed to enjoy being chased and when the dog caught her Gemma would put two paws on the duck's back to hold her. In turn the duck would quite gently peck at the dog's coat or a mild wrestling match would ensue.

The pair became famous in their area of Newton Abbot, Devon, and a scout from Westward Television went to see for himself, resulting in arrangements to travel to Plymouth being made. Gemma was no hassle, she just curled up in the stationwagon and slept. But how to transport a huge duck? A large box was obtained and in went Dillys, but no sooner had the journey started than she got out and settled herself on the lap of Jo, the daughter of the house, and stayed there contented until the arrival at the studio. Then she just meandered around until it was her turn to be 'interviewed'. One would have thought it was something she did every day and she proved a star well-behaved performer and sat meekly until the cameras were on her, then she either groomed the dog or vice versa.

It was excellent viewing, a lovely change from boring humans or so called human 'stars'.

Dillys however, who like a dog comes to the call, has one small fault which rather proves she is of the feminine gender, for she loves jewellery. If a lady wears a bracelet, brooch or even earrings, given the chance, she pecks at them. The earrings are her special delight. In the same way the disc on

Gemma's collar also comes under attack.

She has a good appetite and gets through some 7lb of pellets and grain a week, despite the fact that she is continually on the 'peck' on the lawns and flower beds.

At night Dillys retires to the greenhouse and the dog to the house but first thing every morning there is an affectionate greeting, but only after the bird has completed her ablutions in the small pond which was made for her. Then begins another day's romp with her strange four-legged pal.

She is certainly a very lovely bird that keeps herself beautifully clean and wholesome and as for the dog she is just superb too.

Before the bird came, Gemma took little notice of people or other dogs passing the gate, but she very soon appointed herself Dillys's keeper and a strange dog just passing is vociferously warned off.

— ∞ — ∞ — ∞ — ∞ — ∞ —

Spaniel Mothers Owl Chicks

— ∞ — ∞ — ∞ — ∞ — ∞ —

THE terrible decline of that most beautiful and useful of birds, the barn owl, led to the founding of the New Forest Owl Sanctuary for the breeding and release of birds of prey to the wild.

The barn owl readily breeds in captivity and the chicks are later released in the wild.

The drastic decline of the bird is serious as it used to be an adjunct to every farm and barn as it kept down vermin. Its virtual disappearance has been due to a number of causes which have come together at the same time. The most savage is probably road traffic death and accidents which account for between three and six thousand fatalities each year. Most are caused through them being temporarily blinded by car lights, the owl drops to the ground to recover and is hit by the next vehicle.

On a lesser scale is the buying up of barns to convert to housing. No provision is made in such buildings. Traditional buildings always had a 'pop' hole about twelve inches square so that owls could get in and out to nest and breed.

At the Owl Sanctuary a great help to the humans is Jay, a ten-year-old spaniel, who has adopted a maternal attitude to all the chicks. She guards them and no one she does not know is allowed to touch them. If, as all youngsters do, they annoy her while she is sitting next to the fire she gently picks them up and carries them to the other side of the room, then rushes back. In this way she gets a few minutes rest, before the chick returns to 'Mother'. She sits patiently nestling the fledglings which may number up to six or more.

This great work of conservation goes on and during 1990, fifty-four pairs of the owls went to farms and gamekeeper estates. A breed nucleus of eight pairs were recently sent to Sweden to set up a breeding project there.

The Sanctuary also deals with many other types of owl and maintains a hospital unit for sick and injured birds.

— ∞ — ∞ — ∞ — ∞ — ∞ —

Fisherman Did Not Have to Fib

— ∞ — ∞ — ∞ — ∞ — ∞ —

BRITISH weather certainly proves a perpetual conundrum and in recent years all kinds of birds, animals and fish have wandered far from their normal areas.

Currents and weather have been responsible for many visitors, but by far the most extraordinary was the leatherback turtle discovered dead on a beach near Harlech, Wales. It was by far the largest found in British waters that can be remembered and it is believed it swam from its home either in the Caribbean or North Africa. The theory is that this monster followed thousands of jelly fish to these waters.

The keeper of zoology at the National Museum of Wales collected the turtle and put it in to cold storage to await a taxidermist, so that later it could be put on display.

On examination the turtle was the largest authenticated leatherback ever recorded and had died when it became entangled in whelk fishing lines. It was dead when cut from the winch lines and was washed ashore.

Its total length from nose to tail was 113½in
Dorsal width flipper to flipper 108in
Body depth 37in
Whole weight 2016lb

The magnificent specimen is now on show at the National Museum of Wales, Cathays Park, Cardiff, to which we are indebted for the above information.

— ∞ — ∞ — ∞ — ∞ — ∞ —

Another giant leatherback turtle had better luck off the Cornish coast.

It became ensnared accidentally by a rope and was trapped for a week before it was discovered by a Mullion fisherman. The rope marking a crab pot had become wrapped round one of its flippers. The turtle, 9ft in length, was too large for the fisherman to manage by himself, so the Cornwall Trust for Nature Conservation was called in to help. Experienced divers were taken out to the turtle, five miles off the Lizard. They were half-an-hour underwater until the trapped creature was freed. It kept swimming around flapping its freed flipper.

Once free, it did not just put out to sea, but swam round the boat and even went alongside as if to say thank you before it dived beneath the waves and put out to sea.

This was the twelfth sighting of such a monster in the 1990 season and it is assumed that they followed the jelly fish on which they feed and must have drifted farther north than usual, enticed by the warm weather.

— ∞ — ∞ — ∞ — ∞ — ∞ —

Amy, the turtle, presumed dead for thirteen years, was found alive and well. The soft-backed turtle vanished from Paignton Zoo in 1976.

'After hunting for her for about twelve months she went on our list of missing, presumed dead,' said the zoo official.

'We just assumed she had died, then one of the keepers noticed a small muddy mass walking across the floor of the reptile house. When we cleaned off the mud it was found to be Amy. We were flabbergasted.'

Keeper Dennis Hoare said: 'It looks as if she has been living in the mud in the bottom of a shallow pond for all those years.'

— ∞ — ∞ — ∞ — ∞ — ∞ —

Dolphin Starts a Miracle Cure

— ∞ — ∞ — ∞ — ∞ — ∞ —

IT was a miracle break-through says the grandmother of Matthew, a three-year-old lad from Newton Abbot who suffered from Downs Syndrome and was unable to speak.

As a last resort and without too much hope, he was sent to the marine therapy pioneer Dr David Nathanson at the Dolphin Research Centre in Florida as a result of a newspaper article.

The toddler's first word came after just two hours in the water with Anna, the name of the bottle-nosed dolphin. Matthew watched it quite fascinated and took to the water with his new playmate with enthusiasm.

At the end of three weeks Matthew was able to speak a dozen words, including 'ice' and 'cow', after intensive repetition, using the dolphin to encourage him.

It is hoped he will return to Miami for another visit in a few years time.

It has long been acknowledged that the brain of a dolphin or whale is very high up in the animal world and still these lovely creatures are hounded and slaughtered in hundreds by the Japanese. What a sad world.

— ∞ — ∞ — ∞ — ∞ — ∞ —

Can a Dog Sympathise?

— ∞ — ∞ — ∞ — ∞ — ∞ —

THAT animals, particularly dogs, have feelings and understanding is obvious to people who either own or study them. Even so, dog lovers are occasionally astounded by the degree of sensitivity shown by their pets, sometimes in the most unlikely circumstances. How often, for instance, does a dog in a car make apparent his like or dislike of another on the pavement, even when the car is travelling quite fast and one would have thought that there was no time for reactions!

Hamish was a dour Scotch terrier owned by Mr and Mrs R F Hartill of Nuneaton in Warwickshire. So jealously did he guard the premises that he would not allow either cat or dog to put a nose in the front gate. He would sit at the window for long periods, swaying slightly to and fro – and if a trespasser dared to invade he would go berserk, tearing out of the house with the rugs and mats flying and skidding in his wake. They were rare and brave spirits who managed to stand their ground before such an onslaught.

The family were all the more surprised one day when Hamish was seen to be escorting a woebegone little mongrel up the drive and gently nosing him down to the doormat by the front door. It was all the more amazing because this was his own special holy of holies. Having settled the stranger on to the mat, he then went to recruit human help. This visitor was obviously a stray – dirty, cold, hungry and very, very scared. They took him in and bathed him, Hamish watching approvingly and adding an occasional lick of his own. The stray was then fed from Hamish's bowl and put for the night in Hamish's bed without the slightest protest from him. In due course the dog's owner was found, but Hamish was the courteous host right to the end.

How much perception and understanding? We shall never know, but it was all so out of character that only some deeply embedded instinct could have given rise to such impeccable behaviour.

— ∞ — ∞ — ∞ — ∞ — ∞ —

Mrs and Mrs J W Aldridge of Guildford (Surrey) also had a dog which seemed to be able to work things out in his own way. Not only was Pippin, a corgi, exceptionally intelligent but he seemed to delight in making himself useful. If any member of the family was ill, then Pippin became the messenger and carrier, transporting papers and anything else upstairs to the patient, a job he was prepared to do all day if necessary.

One of his great joys was to accompany his master, who suffered with arthritis, on his walks in the garden. One day on his perambulations, the master dropped his stick. He was unable to bend down to retrieve it but the corgi settled that. First he picked it up and held it towards the man. The corgi, however, was too short and when it was not taken from him he immediately realised why. So up on his hind legs he stood and again proffered the stick which was then high enough to be grasped. Pippin again proved able to think out a new problem and find the right solution.

Just Goats

— ∞ — ∞ — ∞ — ∞ — ∞ —

Woolly Goats

— ∞ — ∞ — ∞ — ∞ — ∞ —

GOATS are becoming increasingly popular all over the country due largely to the fact that they are highly intelligent and playful with a very pronounced sense of fun and certainly an economic proposition for their health-giving milk and in some cases, their woolly, mohair coat. There are many breeds including: British Alpine, British Toggenburg, English, Bagot, Angora, famous and much sought after for their wool, Toggenburg, Anglo Nubian, Saanen, Pygmy, Golden Guernsey etc.

The Angora goat originally came from Turkey, and about 150 years ago some animals were taken to Texas, and also South Africa where they are still commercially farmed in large numbers. Both South Africa and Texas lead the world in the production of quantity and quality of mohair. In the case of Texas, mohair is the second most important product of the state, after oil. More recently Australia and New Zealand have started farming Angoras, and have found them a viable enterprise.

— ∞ — ∞ — ∞ — ∞ — ∞ —

Milly Found a Way

— ∞ — ∞ — ∞ — ∞ — ∞ —

ANOTHER goat story concerns Milly, a white, female kid, and though she lived next door nothing would keep her in her own premises. She would refuse to accept a fence as an obstacle and would somehow get through where there were several goats kept by a neighbour.

There were also several sheep and when fodder was taken to the sheep house, Milly seemed to smell it wherever she was and came at a gallop to get a quick meal. It became a battle of wits to get the fodder to the sheep before Milly got there first.

As time went on she spent more time 'next door' than in her own yard. Then a terrible thing happened. Her owner had tethered her temporarily to a trailer, and unaware of this, someone borrowed the trailer and drove off. She incurred dreadful injuries including almost the loss of one eye, but with expert attention she proved quite indomitable and made an excellent recovery.

Despite doubts, she was able to bring into the world a fine male kid.

Meanwhile her owner had moved to the far end of the village, but Milly would again escape and the owner would phone to say, 'Milly is on her way'. Her arrival was heralded by a sustained bleating at the gate. Her perambulations were however quite self-centred for she had fallen for Smiley, a beautiful male. In due course her owner moved elsewhere and offered Milly as a gift to the owner of the several goats. There were nine of them and at first they gave Milly a bad time, but gradually she was accepted and in due course gave birth to two lovely kids and is now very much part of the family she adopted.

She has proved an incredible milker and has a great love of people. She just accepts everything as it comes and has one of the nicest temperaments possible.

— ∞ — ∞ — ∞ — ∞ — ∞ —

Goats' Coastal Capers

— ∞ — ∞ — ∞ — ∞ — ∞ —

A lady and gentleman who have a herd of goats at Appledore, North Devon, decided one beautiful autumn day to take their charges for a walk along the coastal path to the sand dunes.

It was something they often did as the goats loved such a romp. So loading them into the van they set off on what turned out to be an hilarious morning. It started on a high note when Jura, the half Golden Guernsey and the natural clown of the herd, took station at the rear of the van and pressing her nose tight up against the rear window, pulled faces, to the amusement – or perhaps perturbation is a better word – of the motorists following and those passing.

In due course, the contingent arrived at the narrow coastal path and they all disembarked. Snow, a white Nubian cross Saanen, was the great nanny of the herd and like a pernickety old maid she marshalled the others into single file, strictly in their pecking order and then took station as a rearguard. When all was in order to her satisfaction, she pushed past everyone to take station at the head of the column.

On arrival at the dunes, the goats began a romp. Scrambling up the highest, and running down the other side of the dunes. It was a game that was interspersed by victory jumps on the top. It was a game too, where the one at the top was often besieged by the others trying to dislodge him. After a while the game palled, and the humans who had met two friends played hide and seek with the animals. When the goats made a 'find' they would repeatedly jump high in the air to signal their delight.

The humans tired of this game first and sat down to chat, while the goats browsed around quite peacefully.

Soon afterwards a family of holidaymakers came along and Snow watched them with interest and when they had gone some distance, suddenly took off after them in a frenzied gallop. The herd followed her.

Never having seen her behave like this before, one of the owners in the party ran after her calling, 'Snow', which she rarely failed to heed, but this time she took no notice at all.

By this time the holidaymakers seemed perturbed and began to hurry along. At last, with an obvious fear of the galloping herd, they stopped and huddled together by a dune, fearing the worst. Then the owner came running, still calling the leader. He paused at the group who asked him whether they were wild goats or privately owned, but feeling silence was a golden rule he hurried on after the herd, knowing full well that the visitors thought him completely mad.

The chase went on. One moment the goats were in view, and the next out of sight behind a dune.

At last the path came into view and reassembling her herd into single file order, Snow led off at a sedate pace along the path back to the van.

Snow obviously thought they had been out long enough and decreed that they should get home. She had obviously enjoyed her day out, but enough was enough and she was tired.

Now Jura is the leader of the herd and Snow has her outings with an Arab mare.

It would seem that Snow watched the holidaymakers going in the direction of home and decided to get there first.

— ∞ — ∞ — ∞ — ∞ — ∞ —

Rescued Just in Time

— ∞ — ∞ — ∞ — ∞ — ∞ —

IT is quite astounding the way that animals have the sense to stand by one of their kind when in trouble.

Such a case was that which involved two goats, Fealty and Filigree. They had been browsing with the herd and Filigree got tangled in some wire over a deep ditch.

The grazing area for some twenty goats was extensive, comprising four large fields, an orchard and trees. Wire over a ditch marked the boundary of the farm and grazing area.

Most animals seem to have a built-in alarm clock system and this herd of goats was no exception. When it was time to go home they set off on time to amble back through the woods, but when they arrived, the owner noticed two were missing. She immediately set off to find them and searched the area for some time before she was alerted by a faint bleat. Making her way towards the sound she found Filigree, a very large goat and a 400 gallon milker, was caught in wire and laying on her back in the boundary ditch in great distress, with Fealty anxiously watching. It was she who bleated the alarm. The distressed goat was nearly unconscious and was far too heavy to lift, and even when the wire was disentangled was unable to get to her feet. By dint of massaging her legs, the owner was able to get her up, and she was able to totter home across the fields and through the wood accompanied by the ever watchful Fealty.

Had this goat not stood by the other, there is no doubt that she would have died where she lay.

Filigree was the winner of several challenge certificates and she received a great welcome back to the fold.

— ∞ — ∞ — ∞ — ∞ — ∞ —

The Goats of Lynmouth

— ∞ — ∞ — ∞ — ∞ — ∞ —

AS far back as anyone can remember, there have been Cheviot Goats, one of the oldest English breeds, roaming in the famed Valley of Rocks at Lynton, North Devon. They normally keep themselves very much out of sight but occasionally visitors will see them on the highest of the steep rocks.

Like the apes of Gibraltar, there has always been a local legend that if the goats disappeared disaster would come to the village.

Very occasionally would any of the animals stroll into the small town, but on one occasion a Billy goat with a high aroma forced his way into the Council Chamber while a question of whether the goats should be culled was being discussed.

In 1990-91, a cull became necessary and it was decided to export some of them to Lundy, an island which juts out into the Bristol Channel and which had a dwindling herd.

It was suggested that they would be line bred with the hardy Lundy goats, believed to have been shipped in as prey for tigers planned to be introduced by the island's former owner, Martin Herman in 1935.

The proposal to export some of the Lynton stock was welcomed by the Mayor of Lynton, Mr D Hobbs, who has been responsible for the despatch of the surplus animals as their population began to grow out of control in the late seventies. This was an unpleasant task which was delegated to the Mayor of Lynton after the Billy goat made his surprise appearance in the Council Chamber.

The goat warden, Mr R Warner, a member of the Rare Breeds Survival Trust, planned the shipment to Lundy.

The administrator of Lundy, which is now owned by the Landmark Trust, welcomed the idea.

Lundy is a gigantic mass of granite some three-quarters-of-a-mile long by half-a-mile wide and stands 500ft above sea level. The new goats should be in their element in the new surroundings where they will be used to bolster the declining Lundy goats.

— ∞ — ∞ — ∞ — ∞ — ∞ —

Lucky Indeed

— ∞ — ∞ — ∞ — ∞ — ∞ —

AN Angora goat, one of three triplets, is named Bonus – she should have been called Lucky for she is lucky to be alive.

She was a tiny goat kid standing only 7in high and weighing just 2lb. Strange to say, the mother ignored and abandoned her new offspring. Mrs Fraser of East Devon who has kept goats for years, took the three kids into her kitchen to keep them warm and bottle feed them.

Other occupants of the farm are two fine alsatians, Rambo and Ria, and Rambo particularly sensed something was wrong and decided to lend a hand. Directly the kids had their bottles, Rambo would lick them all over for a special clean-up, and paying particular attention to their faces which had very thorough treatment.

It was a duty that both dogs maintained until the kids could be put in the field with the other fully grown goats. Even months after, Rambo kept a watchful eye on the tiny one. Now except for being shorter in the leg than usual Bonus is a fine specimen and almost too heavy to pick up. Mrs Frazer has never known any goat to refuse its kids, especially such a small one.

Mrs Frazer who keeps goats, dogs, cats and horses is a great believer in letting them all mix in together and certainly they can teach humanity a lesson to live and let live (see picture on back of jacket).

As for the two alsatians, they are superb guard dogs with a bark that would scare anyone, but they really are 'softees' – especially when it comes to young goats.

$$- \infty - \infty - \infty - \infty - \infty -$$

Topsy's Journey

$$- \infty - \infty - \infty - \infty - \infty -$$

GOATS frequently hit the headlines. They are useful animals in many circumstances and in the Western Isles of Scotland they frequently provide the milk, for often the pasture is not good enough to keep a cow. It was for this purpose that Topsy, a fine goat, became involved in a 600-mile journey from Peterborough, in Northamptonshire, to the Isle of Skye.

A crofter was living at Point of Sleat, seven miles from any other village on Skye. His three little girls – Elsbeth, Emma and Morag – needed milk, and as they possessed no cow it was difficult to obtain. Then on the mainland, the crofter's friend Ian Holdsworthy saw a goat advertised for £10. He thought of the island family and snapped it up. Then came the problem – how to transport his purchase all the way from Peterborough to Skye.

With the goat on a lead, and carrying a bag of hay as sustenance for the journey, Ian Holdsworthy bought a ticket at

Peterborough railway station. Airily he explained his charge away as being an African mountain dog. The first change was at Grantham, where unfortunately Topsy forgot herself and butted a railway porter. The journey continued. At Fort William she was duly admired by other passengers and at Mallaig, Inverness-shire, she was milked. Except for the one misdemeanour at Grantham, she was a perfect little lady and an ideal passenger. Eventually Ian Holdsworthy and his 'African mountain dog' took the ferry to Skye, and the long trip was over.

The three little girls were delighted to welcome Topsy even before they tasted her milk.

W ORLD OF THE H ORSE

— ∞ — ∞ — ∞ — ∞ — ∞ —

The Queen's Horses

— ∞ — ∞ — ∞ — ∞ — ∞ —

ONE of the most exciting events at a military tattoo or tournament, and one which exudes glamour, tradition and thrills, is the musical drive of the King's Troop, Royal Horse Artillery (RHA). To see the six horses of each team galloping fully stretched across an arena and performing an intricate weaving pattern is certainly a joy. It is a rigorous test of the drivers' skill, where in an average display some two miles are covered and the gun and limber weigh a ton and a half. Little wonder, therefore, that the demands for the services of the King's Troop outnumber the engagements that they can accept.

The history of the King's Troop goes back to the Napoleonic period, when a brigade of the Royal Horse Artillery was stationed in some old warehouses at St James's Park. In 1811, the decision was taken to move the brigade to St John's Wood and a plan was laid down to build a barracks there. With Napoleon safely beaten, however, the area was abandoned by the military. Only a few years elapsed before King George IV had to find a new site for the royal mews, then occupying the site upon which the National Gallery now stands. So a new riding house was built at St John's Wood, at that time with open fields and farmland on three sides. The barracks in 'the Wood' has had many changes since then.

The old buildings gave good service but were completely rebuilt in 1971, and now house The King's Troop RHA. The Troop was redesignated in 1947 from the 'Riding Troop RHA' and is a ceremonial unit, part of the Household Troops. Few Londoners appreciate that there are barracks and stables in a suburb so close to the city's very heart. The new buildings are thoroughly modern and it is here that The King's Troop trains and operates.

The Troop is commanded by a major and has a strength of seven officers, including a veterinary officer, 185 soldiers and 111 horses. An entirely self-contained unit, it is organised into a Troop Headquarters and three sections, each commanded by a subaltern, with two guns per section. In addition to the gunners and drivers who appear in public and are responsible for grooming and feeding the horses, cleaning their harness and the guns, there is a saddler's shop which repairs the 'tack' – and indeed, makes much of it – and the farrier's shop where the horses are shod. The farriers are also trained in minor veterinary treatment. There is a pharmacy with a veterinary officer and veterinary sergeant; horsebox and Land Rover drivers, clerks for the offices, storemen, carpenters and cooks – and all are knit together to form the team which produces the results to be seen on parade.

Wherever ceremonial duties are to be performed, be they pulling a gun carriage for a royal or military funeral, a royal salute, or the dash and glamour of a musical drive, the horses and men of The King's Troop are in demand. When a salute is to be fired in Hyde Park, the Troop is accorded a privilege normally enjoyed only by Her Majesty the Queen, the gates at Marble Arch are opened to allow them access.

The horses, selected to a prescribed standard, come from the Republic of Ireland. They may be from four to six years old, stand up to sixteen hands and are either light or dark bays, browns or blacks. Certainly they have to stand up to hard work. On attaining the age of fifteen they are subjected to a careful review each year, and it reflects well on the care bestowed upon them that there are horses still on the strength which have attained twenty years of age.

Horses are issued from the Remount Depot, Melton Mowbray, and they, with soldiers of the Troop, are ridden, assessed and trained for draught and riding work. Six horses make up each team and the leading pair have to be large and bold animals for theirs is the heaviest share of the pulling. The driver rides the left-hand horse, which is known as the ride horse; his counterpart is the hand horse. Then, slightly smaller than the leaders, are the ride and hand centres – and finally, the smallest of all, those closest to the gun-carriage, the ride and hand wheelers. Each team is colour matched.

When new horses have reached a given point in training, they are placed in the centre of the team so that they can gain confidence from the others. It may take nine months before a horse can be judged to have completed the training. Generally they adapt to the routine very quickly. Forced training is useless; it takes too much out of an animal and it is accepted that the quicker they learn the quicker they forget, for a horse is a nervous and sensitive animal.

The riding school at the St John's Wood barracks is certainly one of the finest military establishments in the country. Built in 1824 at a cost of £5,712.4s.9d, it measures a little over 56m (184ft) in length by 19.5m (64ft) wide. The timber roof rising to 7.3m (24ft) is magnificent in its design and span, and here the Riding Master trains both horses and men. The four walls of the school are fitted with large mirrors which enable the riders to observe themselves at any angle. A great help in the correction of faults.

While every one of the hundred-odd horses has individual traits and a personality of its own, occasionally a real character emerges. Every animal has its name but invariably in some way it earns a nickname as well. There was, for instance, Western – known as Spud – who, if given a lump of sugar, would follow a soldier all around the barracks hoping for more. However, he did not like trumpets and if anybody went into his stall with one, he would have it out of their hands at once.

There is Ronald, a nine-year-old centre horse in a gun team. Standing fifteen hands and as versatile as any horse can be, he has featured in show jumping, horse trials and hunting, apart from his place in a gun-carriage team. High Hat is a mare of sixteen years. Twice she has been awarded the blue riband of the Royal Tournament. She, too, serves in a team and has also been successful at point-to-point meetings and combined training.

An altogether different character is Hancock. Who knows – perhaps it is the indignity of his nickname, Stumpy, which causes him to bite and kick without provocation if anyone comes too near? Feeding time is an exception and on parade he is magnificent. Once in the full panoply of his show harness, he is the proudest show-off of them all. Discussion of his peculiarities near his stall will produce a prima-donna-like display of temperament, as if to prove the truth of his reputation. Without doubt, horses, like humans have minds of their own.

Lasting fame has been achieved by several of the horses of the Royal Horse Artillery. Jones and Joubert were lead horses at Aldershot before World War I. They went to war and served up to the end. In all those years they were never sick or sorry. On their return to England in 1919, they were taken to Aldershot where they had formerly been stabled. Jones was let loose on the square and the men watched in amazement as he nonchalantly made off in the direction of the stables – not only to the stables but to the very stall he had occupied before the war. Not a bad feat of memory after six year's absence!

Another horse was David, who saw service in the South African war and then World War I, where he took part in all the principal battles, including Mons. The fiercest gunfire never made him flinch; he wore four wound stripes and was entitled to six medals and awards. Truly an old soldier in every sense of the word.

The story is told, too, of one pair who worked together in the team and were inseparable, even sharing a box together. Tempers only flared when they were separated.

Generally speaking, all who volunteer for The King's Troop love horses. Indeed it must be so, for their day begins before 6am each morning and ends at about 5pm. It is hard work and often calls for considerable self sacrifice. It is significant, too, that there are more dogs as pets, ranging from alsatians to Yorkshire terriers, than in most similar establishments.

The Troop is well represented at eventing, hunter trials and show jumping competitions. It holds its own point-to-point race open to all ranks, and every soldier has an opportunity to compete in the Troop's own mounted sports competitions throughout the year. Furthermore, they have produced several international competitors; three members of the Troop have represented this country in three different Olympics, and there have been many others who have competed successfully at national level.

In 1973, for the first time in over 200 years, The King's Troop mounted the Queen's Life Guard in Whitehall. A five mile walk from the barracks and then standing still on guard duty for an hour was a far cry from galloping salutes, but they came through with flying colours.

Many fine animals are to be found in the stalls today: Elvis, a mere youngster of five years, Leopard (Tich), who delights in grabbing his groom's cap and throwing it over his back, and Halfpenny, Revenge, Rapture, Royalty, Boadicea, Beaufort, Harlequin and scores of others.

Their food consists of oats, bran, nuts, chopped hay and in winter, boiled barley and linseed, fed hot. Occasionally greens and molasses. The amount of feed depends on the work they are doing.

In the barracks they have their daily exercise, early each morning, are groomed and then rest. But when they are on view to the public at a Tournament, Tattoo or Ceremonial occasion, they hold their heads high. The immaculate turn-out of both men and horses is only possible with continuous training, hard work and constant effort to improve, if possible, upon even the high standard that they always achieve.

— ∞ — ∞ — ∞ — ∞ — ∞ —

The Royal Mews

— ∞ — ∞ — ∞ — ∞ — ∞ —

TO enter the Royal Mews at Buckingham Palace is to take a step back in time, for the great quadrangle within the gates is flanked by stables and coach houses which seem to (and indeed do) belong to another age. The horses remain to remind us of the unhurried pace of life before the internal combustion engine arrived and in two or three decades took control of our way of life.

From the time of Richard II the Royal Mews was at Charing Cross. Up to 1537 it was used exclusively for keeping falcons, but Henry VIII replaced the birds with a stud of horses.

Buckingham House, now the palace, was purchased by George III and since his time horses have been kept at the present Royal Mews with its entrance on to Buckingham Palace Road. Certainly they are now among the finest stables anywhere; they occupy three sides of the square to the west and north, while on the opposite side are housed the magnificent coaches used on State occasions.

The horses today are of various breeds, but the Cleveland Bays hold pride of place, supplemented mostly by Oldenburg horses from Germany. These are the heaviest of the German warm-blooded breed. Large, well-made animals, they have a well muscled neck and shoulder, a compact muscular back, and short, strong legs with plenty of bone. In addition the Oldenburgers have a very good temperament and a better action in harness than most.

There are some thirty carriage horses of various ages at the mews; among them is Montreal, a Windsor Grey aged twenty-two. At the other end of the scale are the youngsters of two and three years who are being trained for the future.

An interesting item in the stables is a guardsman's uniform complete with bearskin. It occupies a stand in a prominent position and sometimes the grooms wear it when attending to the horses, familiarising them with figures they meet on most occasions.

The Windsor Greys, which always have the lion's share of attention at royal events, draw the Queen's carriages and were used for the coronation of King George VI and the present Queen. They are not a special breed but grey horses were always kept at Windsor since Victorian times, and only in 1936 were they moved to London. Their name comes from their long use at Windsor.

The harness at the mews is bewildering in both its quantity and its varying styles. To clean it all would occupy a man for two months. Most of the harness is embellished with solid brass bosses. There are eight sets of red Moroccan State harness which was made in 1834 and is used for the horses drawing the gold coach. Each set weighs 110lb and all is richly ornamented with gilt ormolu. There are various sets of special harness for use with other State coaches. Two sets of blue State harness were made in the reign of George III

The magnificent gold state coach was built in 1762 and weighs four tons. It is 7.3m (24ft) in length, over 2.4m (8ft) wide and 3.6m (12ft) high, and is gilded all over. It has been used for every coronation since George IV's and was last used during the Silver Jubilee year (1977) on the state drive to St Paul's Cathedral. This is the vehicle to which eight postillion horses are harnessed and the only coach in the Royal Mews which has to proceed at a walking pace.

At the northern end of the mews are the motor cars, which have largely displaced the horses in most State occasions.

On every state occasion a farrier from the mews is somewhere close by. The horses are shod at three-weekly intervals and it is rare for a horse to lose a shoe, but it has been known. Should this happen, then at the first pause in the proceedings a cold shoe hinged to fit any horse is fitted as a temporary measure, for the show must go on.

No other country in the world is capable of holding a State occasion on the scale of impressiveness that Britain can achieve. Today it is a far cry from the coronation procession of Queen Victoria, when more than fifty coaches were used to accommodate the VIPs alone. Nevertheless, on these special occasions when all is glitter and dignity, it is largely the beautifully caparisoned horses of the Royal Mews that make it so. At such events the horse really comes into its own.

— ∞ — ∞ — ∞ — ∞ — ∞ —

The Pride and Dignity of Shire Horses

— ∞ — ∞ — ∞ — ∞ — ∞ —

TO my mind the most magnificent of British animals is the heavy horse. Huge, handsome, of placid nature and tremendous dignity they are with their shining coats always an eye-catcher. Fortunately, by reason of their strength, stamina and adaptability they are making a come back after the fear in the twenties that the breed would die out having seemingly lost the battle with the petrol engine.

There are four breeds of heavy horse, the Clydesdale, Suffolk Punch, Percheron and the Shire – the heaviest of them all.

The ancestors of these heavy breeds were most certainly the war horses of medieval times when strength and stamina were essential if only to carry the extra weight of the armour of horse and rider.

Centuries later they were bred for the vital part they were

146

to play in the industrial revolution in agriculture, pulling barges and transport generally.

Today, again, they may be seen in cities pulling the heavy loads, particularly those for breweries who find that for short hauls in crowded streets they prove both economical and ideal for a variety of jobs to which they quickly adapt. Despite the advent of the tractor, there are many purposes on the farm where they are useful.

Fortunately over the years every effort has been made to establish a uniformity of type, character and appearance, and this has been largely achieved by the Shire Horse Society which was established in 1878.

In the twenties the breed numbered some two million but numbers declined rapidly to a few thousand. Since then, fortunately, the heavy horse is again much in demand and their numbers are increasing.

The National Shire Horse Centre

These lovely animals may be seen to the best advantage at the National Shire Horse Centre at Yealmpton near Plymouth, where over the last few years a very fine complex has been built up.

The mares carry a foal for eleven months and usually the birth takes place without human aid. The new foal is 10 or 11 hands high and from then on grows at the rate of one inch a week, reaching maturity in five years, with an average life expectancy of twenty-five.

A full grown shire weighs a ton or more and can easily pull a weight of many tons. It stands an average of 17 hands, or nearly 6ft high at the shoulder, and one particular specimen King, stands well over 18 hands and is magnificent.

Any human with a very good appetite is said to 'eat like a horse', and one can see how this came about for in winter months a fully grown shire manages to consume two bales of hay and 20lb of oats each day.

Their energy and strength is amazing and perhaps the best example is if ploughing, for instance, a one-and-a-quarter acre field it entails walking fourteen miles each day.

The story of the centre is in itself interesting for it was created in 1978, evolving from a hobby of Mr Tony Flower. Now his five sons and one daughter all work at the centre.

Visitors may walk through spacious and airy stables at Yealmpton and will be greeted by these beautiful animals which like to know what is going on.

The complex has been built around the original farmhouse, a Devon Longhouse which is 200 years old, and apart from a variety of interests, shire horses are bred, some of which are exported to the United States, Australia and New Zealand.

The centre has its own registered farrier, an ex-Household Cavalry man, who formerly served as groom and farrier to the Queen's Drum horses. Also there is a full time harness maker and wheelwright.

Twice a day all the horses (usually about thirty) are paraded in the spacious arena which seats some 5,000, and another is in course of construction. As each horse enters the arena a running commentary is given. The various types of harness and the whys and wherefores are also dealt with.

Other displays include those at the falconry centre by an expert who has built up his own collection of birds of prey. There are some magnificent specimens including an Eagle Owl, Buzzard, Mexican Harris Hawk, Kestrel and Launer. It all started as a result of bird watching as a boy.

While horses steal the show at this centre, there are a number of other interesting sections open to the visitor including a newly added butterfly centre. Equipped with many special plants, species of butterflies from all over the world fly around.

Naturally there is a great demand from shows, carnivals etc, to show off the horses and in the museum are splendid examples of harness. One set of Cornish decorated harness still worn on special occasions by one horse, comprises 1,500 individual brasses, plumes and bells which were always a feature of Cornish decoration. The weight of this fine array exceeds 200lb and incidentally it takes one person three days to clean. It says something for the intense pride of the older generation of those who worked with the horse.

This Shire Horse Centre is all embracing for there is a Shire Horse School, working holidays for those who love and wish to learn about horses, a pets centre, with animals ranging from dwarf goats down to chipmunks, and a bird sanctuary. There are also nature walks. Altogether the ideal setting for animals – so different from those always kept in confined spaces.

The West Country Shire Horse Trust, a registered charity, is based at Yealmpton and encourages the breeding and working of the shire on farms. It also saves horses which have been neglected or marked down for slaughter.

A noteable success story in this respect was the rescue of a twenty-year-old shire from slaughter. Margaret, a mare, was suffering from rheumatism and at first showed no sign of recovery. Then she was turned out to the fields with the hope that nature would help. It did and miraculously she produced a fine healthy foal which is at the centre today.

Dogs – How They Serve

— ∞ — ∞ — ∞ — ∞ — ∞ —

How They Serve

— ∞ — ∞ — ∞ — ∞ — ∞ —

In the Cause of Law and Order

Today we acknowledge that dogs give a great service to man in the keeping of law and order. It is now commonplace to see dogs with their handlers assisting at many types of police enquiry, but it was not until about 1950 that police forces in Britain began to accept, train and rely on dogs for certain aspects of their work.

In Lincolnshire, one of the largest counties in Britain, the constabulary was one of the first to set up a special dog-training department, and the story is an interesting one. It began in 1948 when Constable D.C. Needham used his own two alsatians from time to time in certain aspects of his job. Recognising their potential, he suggested to his chief constable that a police dog section be set up to assist the force.

The rapid growth of dog sections is demonstrated by the fact that at this time the chief constable had never heard of police dogs as such. Eventually it was through the influence or Sir Joseph Simpson (late Commissioner of the Metropolitan Police) that the idea was generally accepted. Constable Needham set to work. He went as an observer to a course in Surrey, where representatives of five or six other police forces were on the same errand.

The official police dog section in Lincoln was set up in 1955. Labradors, dobermanns, alsatians and a bloodhound were very soon recruited, and over the years the assistance of the dogs has proved of inestimable value in helping to combat and prevent crime. It is generally agreed that police work dealing with the complexities of twentieth-century crime would be much more difficult without them.

It has taken years of trial and error to arrive at an assessment of which breed is most suitable for general purposes, and, indeed, different breeds are favoured by different police forces. At Lincoln all the dogs on the total strength of twenty-six are alsatians with the exception of three labradors, two explosive search dogs and one drug detection dog. The alsatian (or German Shepherd) has proved beyond doubt to be the best all round working dog for police purposes. Some indication of the high standard demanded is the fact that no more than one per cent of all alsatians finally make the grade. The very large percentage of failure is in the opinion of many experts, including Dennis Needham (now retired Inspector), largely due to indiscriminate breeding producing highly nervous and unreliable progeny. Alsatians are dogs of great adaptability and those considered suitable for training usually measure up to the many necessary requirements, one of the most important being unquestionable intelligence. They are consequently largely used by the police, the RAF and the Army, in mountain-rescue work and general guard duties, as guide dogs for the blind, for sheep and cattle herding and in connection with the latest scourge on the calendar of crimes – drug trafficking.

Today the training centre of the Lincolnshire Constabulary is in the hands of Sergeant Ken Christer who worked with Dennis Needham for many years as a constable dog handler and then Sergeant trainer. He took charge of training dogs in Lincolnshire when Dennis retired in 1981. He has since handled three alsatians and a labrador Sam, who he trained in drug detection.

The training programme is tough and all-embracing for all the twenty-one men, one policewoman and the animals. An eight-hour stint on the training grounds with the wind sweeping across the flat Lincolnshire countryside can be a test of stamina in itself.

A high standard is required of the dog handlers, who are

all volunteers. After the basic training period of thirteen weeks, the handlers begin to form an affinity with their animal who becomes a constant companion. Once a dog has been allocated to a handler, the pair love, train and work together, the dog living at the handler's home when off-duty. The average training day commences at 8.15am but the handlers are on call virtually twenty-four hours a day. Usually the beat follows normal routine, the peak hours being 8pm to 3am.

Although the history of the dog as a domestic animal can be traced back to the early Bronze Age, the German shepherd dog (or alsatian, as we know it) originated in Germany towards the end of the last century, and was at that time bred and trained primarily for working with sheep. Sergeant Christer points out that a dog is still basically a pack animal and by and large lives by the rules which have controlled the pack for thousands of years. There is always a leader who directs the activities of the pack, and in the domestic scene the dog looks upon his master as the 'leader' of his 'pack'. This explains why, in family life, a dog may become confused when given orders by several different leaders; whereas the dog would always obey his master's command, an order from a less-favoured person often goes unheeded and the dog's confusion can result in a lack of response or even some animosity towards a particular person.

Furthermore, in training care has to be taken to avoid confusing the dog. Orders must be given clearly, for any indecision on the part of the handler may result in misunderstanding and a breakdown of the necessary rapport between dog and master.

The basic training programme contains five main obedience exercises and these are concerned first with oral command and secondly with visual command, the latter being necessary when the dog is out of earshot or, perhaps, upwind of the handler. A thirteen week basic training course works wonders and the standard of near perfection attained by the dogs in such a period is amazing. One of the five obedience exercises includes the 'send-away' in which the dog is sent away from its handler in a specific direction and in the straightest possible line. After reaching the required distance or particular spot, which can be up to 180–275m (200–300yd) away, the dog is commanded to stay. After a short pause, the dog is redirected either to the left or the right, until it eventually reaches another position when it is again instructed to stay. The exercise is then completed when the dog is recalled to its handler, thereby completing a triangle and covering a distance of approximately 450m (500yd). The commands can be either visual or oral.

An integral part of the training is to teach the dog, while on patrol, to communicate to its handler anything alien in any particular area. It is taught to indicate in no uncertain manner, usually by barking, that there is something to be looked into. The handler releases the dog who makes off to the spot where his senses tell him there is something 'different' that requires investigation. Then his duty is to stand guard and, by barking, direct his handler to his 'find'. A wide variety of objects are used during training, and an old motor-tyre carried across a field and placed in a covert is a typical example. By using its keen sense of smell, the dog is able to acknowledge an object carrying an alien scent. Some amazing finds and subsequent arrests have been made by the dog's awareness of this alien item in an unusual place.

Sergeant Christer believes that in tracking, the animal requires 75 per cent concentration and only 25 per cent ability. This is understandable when it is realised that a dog's sense of smell is at least 60-70 per cent greater than that of the keenest human nose.

The agility training is not only a test of the fitness of the dog, but of control and timing. The dogs make little of an almost standing jump to scramble over an obstacle up to 2m (7ft) high, while they can jump a series of small fences in one bound covering a good 3m (10ft).

The intelligence of the animals is best illustrated when they track or search and eventually come up with a wrongdoer.

Their job is to get to the man, often well in advance of the handler, and then to stand guard and, by barking, guide him to the spot. If the quarry stands still all is well, but immediately he moves the dog will go into attack. The majority of people are right-handed and this is normally the arm which carries a weapon. The dog is, therefore, trained to act accordingly. When the handler is able to catch up with the suspect, the dog's job is by no means finished. He must guard the suspect while he is being searched and then take station between the suspect and his handler during escort. In this way the dog cannot be kicked, nor can the suspect easily turn and attack the man arresting him. Trained to react to gunfire, this is fortunately something few dogs have to face.

In training, a man with a thickly padded right arm makes a determined attempt to escape from the dog. The dog acts aggressively until the man submits; then the animal will circle him, intent, watchful and positioned ready to resume the attack immediately. 45kg (100lb) of dog launched against a man is formidable, quite apart from the teeth, and further struggle once the dog has caught up with a suspect is rare. Only one dog in the force has been badly injured; he was hit over the head with an iron bar.

An amusing story is told of two dogs, which perhaps illustrates the difference between their breeds. One was an alsatian, the other a dobermann, and as part of their training for trials they had to search for a man and then guard him until the handler's arrival. The man, for his part, had to offer the dog food – which, of course, the dog should not accept. The alsatian did the job perfectly; the other came up to the man who offered food and, to the disgust of the trainers, the animal both accepted and ate it. Having enjoyed the repast, the dog then sprang in, attacked the man and tore his clothes. It may have been counter to the rules, but few can decry the thought processes of the animal.

The dogs are continually used in cases which otherwise would not be solved.

Here are a few cases which prove the point: Police dog

Boris and his handler were called from their home address to a lorry taken from Grimsby docks and abandoned at Caenby Corner. Two youths had been seen to run from the vehicle. On his arrival at the scene the dog handler put Boris to work around the vehicle. He picked up a track which led to a wood. He continued to track through the wood and into open farmland diagonally towards the main road. He then tracked across two large fields to a stack of bales – the dog circled the bales and then made towards some nearby farm buildings. These buildings turned out to be cattle sheds and contained a large number of cattle.

Due to this, assistance was summoned by radio for a physical search by Task Force Officers. Boris's handler positioned himself and his dog in the open fields. As the Task Force Officers commenced a search two youths broke cover running towards the handler and his dog, they stood still when challenged and were promptly arrested.

The dog had tracked for just over one hour and had covered a distance of approximately four miles.

Operational Dogs

The dogs continue to be used to good effect operationally with good results all round.

The dog handler and police dog Kurt produced a very good result. Three offenders were disturbed by returning occupants during a dwelling house burglary on the outskirts of Gainsborough, Lincolnshire. The offenders were pursued across fields and eventually arrested. On arrest they were not in possession of any property and gave no information as to its whereabouts.

Kurt and his handler were called in and commenced a search of an area 2–3 miles in length of the approximate route taken. The team had been searching for about fifty minutes across pasture land and ploughed fields when they arrived at a group of derelict farm buildings much overgrown with weeds and thorn bushes. The dog showed interest at one group of thorn bushes but had difficulty gaining access. The handler succeeded in getting his dog across the bushes and commenced a search of the undergrowth. Over a period of about twenty minutes the dog retrieved a total of twenty-two separate items of jewellery valued at £1,805.

The property was identified as being stolen from the dwelling house, and apart from one ring which was not found the complete haul was recovered by police dog Kurt.

This was particularly pleasing to the lady of the house as it included her engagement and eternity rings which could not be replaced.

On report of a prowler at the County Hospital Car Park at 3am a dog handler attended and commenced to search the area with police dog Guy. After about twenty-five minutes the dog inspected some bushes and retrieved a large plastic bag containing several large catering size tins of food. Approximately five minutes later the officer saw a twenty-year-old man walking from the old part of the hospital towards the car park. Not being satisfied with his answers on being questioned, he arrested the man on suspicion. It was then found that a burglary had been committed at the hospital canteen; further items of food were found at the offender's home when searched. He subsequently admitted the offence and was charged with burglary.

At 1.35am the burglar alarm was activated at a club on the outskirts of Lincoln. The dog handler attended, parked his vehicle about 200yd away from the premises and approached with his dog on foot, across waste ground at the rear of the premises. When about 150–200yd away he saw the silhouette of a male walking away from the premises. When challenged, the man ran towards the nearby allotments. Police dog Guy was sent in pursuit in the darkness. After about thirty seconds the constable heard a crash and screaming. On joining his dog he found the man was on the ground with police dog Guy holding onto his harm. The twenty-seven-year-old man was arrested. The handler then searched the premises which had been burgled and found a flick knife. Enquiries found the man was wanted for a stabbing incident earlier that week. He was subsequently charged with burglary and assault.

When the dogs come to retirement age, which can vary from seven to ten years old, depending on the individual animal, they are allowed to retire into the handler's family home. They may not be fit enough for the demanding role of a police dog, but still enjoy a good walk, just reward for a dedicated friend who has been willing to lay his life on the line for his master. Unfortunately many dogs in the British Police Service have done just that. Criminals can be very unscrupulous but many officers lives have been saved by their loyal companion.

Drugs and Explosives

The venue is a large disused aircraft hangar. It is packed with boxes, bales, sacks, machinery, wooden frames and a thousand and one other odds and ends. Avenues separate the lines of goods. Somewhere in this conglomeration of items a piece of cannabis is hidden, a piece no longer than the filter of a tipped cigarette. To the human nose, it is devoid of smell.

An unfortunate sign of the times is the use of explosive search dogs by every police force in the country. The dogs are not just used for actual bomb threats but every day to clear routes and venues for royal and VIP visits. Many Cabinet Ministers, ex-Ministers and MPs are under threat from various terrorist organisations.

Due to the serious consequences of failure in this work, the standard required from these dogs is very demanding. The teams are in fact licensed when trained and a further test takes place every year. If the team or handler and dog is found lacking the licence to search is withdrawn until a test is passed. The dogs are trained to detect all the many types of explosive substances and train continuously, although machines are in existence that will detect certain explosives at close range. It is still admitted by the scientific experts in this that 'Nothing is as good as a dog'. This is a quote from a top scientist at a research establishment.

Some years ago, the author was privileged to see Bonny at

work, a liver-and-white springer spaniel, the first of her breed to be used for this special purpose. Accompanied by her handler, the dog had her head pointed in the direction where a search was required. A pat and a whispered 'Zu' (search) and Bonny was off, tail waging furiously, eyes alert, nose to the ground. After covering the general area she fussed as she approached a sack. Then she made efforts to tip it over, her handler stepped in to pull it over. The dog pounced then looked up enquiring as if to say, 'There you are, is that what you are looking for?' And with a last wag of the tail, wandered off and took no further notice. Her job was done.

This experiment was repeated in several ways, including placing a tin containing cannabis tight down between some brushwood jumps. The relative ease of discovery was always the same.

Bonny set the example as many police forces have since adopted the breed especially for explosive and drug detection.

Sometimes dogs are used at customs check-points at the ports. The ingenuity of the traffickers knows no bounds. Small quantities may be smuggled in a car hub-cap or somewhere on the chassis and are often secreted in luggage, and this is where the dogs are so valuable. A dog has only to pass down a line of people in a queue to be able to intimate to his handler that something or somebody is worth further investigation.

Their sense of smell is quite fantastic. It enables them to locate a piece of cannabis no larger than a pinhead. Moreover, if the drug has been smoked and the ash dropped into a tray, even though it is quickly emptied, the dog can still indicate decisively that 'there was cannabis here'. The faintest such trail, once indicated, can be followed up by the forensic laboratories, usually with damaging results for the offender. When a raid has taken place, it has been known for the offenders to burn joss sticks and plant other substances in an endeavour to put the dogs off the scent – but to no avail.

On one occasion the police suspected that drugs were

being stored or used in a billet occupied by servicemen. A dog was called in, at first with no result; but he seemed loath to leave one room and kept going back to a record player. So certain was the handler that the dog sensed something that the player was eventually stripped down piece by piece, and sure enough a tiny plastic bag containing heroin was found hidden in the working parts.

The Lincolnshire forces most recent drug dog, Sam, handled by Sgt Ken Christer had a similar find, though just one of the many in his career. Sam indicated strongly at a stereo speaker. To put officers and dog off the scent the occupier of the premises had immediately produced a small amount of cannabis and admitted 'That's all I've got'. After Sam's indication the speaker was dismantled and more small blocks of cannabis resin were found sealed in cellophane which in turn were sealed in an envelope which was hidden in the foam interior stuffing of the speaker.

In Bonny's day the dogs were only trained to find cannabis. This training has now been extended to include heroin, cocaine and all the many amphetamine based drugs.

It has been suggested in some circles that the dogs become addicted and this is why they find them. This is absolute rubbish says Sgt Christer. The incentive for the dog is a play article, his reward after a find. A dog addicted to drugs would be the same as a human, useless!

It is generally accepted that the drug traffic can only be contained by the use of these lively, clever and conscientious dogs. Indeed a far cry from, 'Why police dogs?'

One of the two dogs with which former Inspector Needham started was Saracen, or Cent as he was more commonly called. He was possibly the nearest to the perfect police dog that can be achieved. Not only did he often work on his own initiative, but in the show ring and competitive field his record was amazing. He was Working Trials Champion, won the National Police Dog Trials, the Police Dog of the Year and achieved much else. One of his more remarkable arrests was made following people who had escaped from a remand home. Cent picked up the trail in the grounds and followed it along a nearby river. He went on and on. When the escapees moved inland again and made across a series of fields, the dog was hot on their trail. The handler, near to exhaustion, let the dog off the leash to carry on but meanwhile did his best to keep up. Eventually he saw, several fields away, the heads of the two men just above the corn. Making towards them was the alsatian. The dog was discernible only by the movement in the corn, but, as an aid to his bearings and to keep his quarry in sight as well as following the scent, he would periodically jump high above the corn, fix his position and then, satisfied he was on the right course, travel on relentlessly, never minding that his handler was a mile or so behind. At last he caught up with his quarry. He went into the attack and knocked one of the men down. The other, believing that discretion was the better part of valour, gave up. Cent stood guard patiently until his handler arrived to make the arrests. It was a classic case. The dog had kept his nose to the scent, free-tracked, used his eyes as an additional aid and, having made his capture, stood guard barking to guide the handler to the spot.

Cent was quite fantastic too on indication. His instinct seemed to enable him to discriminate which smells were odd or in the wrong place. Once he was passing some shops with his handler, when suddenly he indicated that something was odd. He sniffed around one shop, then trekked off down an alley to a back entrance, stopping at a pair of heavy, double gates. Access was made, and in a corner was a pile of stolen property. There was literally nothing to indicate to a man on the beat that anything unusual was on the premises. How the dog picked up an alien scent from the main road was and still is a complete mystery.

Cent lived to a good age of thirteen-and-a-half years, and for eleven of them served conscientiously and courageously in his line of duty.

There was also Jamie, one of the first alsatians used at Lincoln, who demonstrated and proved, against current belief, that it is possible to track over stagnant water. The 'skin' on the water still retains enough scent for a keen-nosed dog.

Inspector Needham was possibly the only policeman whose qualifications enabled him to be in demand as a judge for the Regional and National Police Dog Working Trials, Kennel Club Championship Trials, Obedience Feats and Breeds. Moreover, he serves on the Home Office Advisory Committee on police dogs and is a popular lecturer. His devotion to his dogs and their handlers had to be seen to be believed, and it is a job which gave little respite. He is virtually always on duty, for members of the public from a wide area never go to him for information about their animals in vain.

His knowledge was in constant demand, not only in this country but also overseas. He was the guest of the South African Alsatian Association as a judge and adviser. He found the members of the Association extremely enthusiastic, though the standard has some way to go before it reaches the British level. Of course, the work the dogs are called upon to do there is very different. Police dogs are used primarily for bush tracking of native criminals, and frequently the dog masters (handlers) are away following a scent for days at a time. The landscape is virtually devoid of roads, people or vehicles, so that the scent will lie unsullied for perhaps twenty-four hours after a man has passed and in a high proportion of cases the native is tracked back to his own village. Sometimes on such treks dogs are interchanged, making it possible to follow the scent for perhaps fifty miles or more at a stretch.

It is estimated that there are some 2,000 police dogs working in the United Kingdom.

Mules – Lovable Creatures

— ∞ — ∞ — ∞ — ∞ — ∞ —

THEY are brave, patient, persevering, calm, cheerful, resilient, intelligent, sensible, sensitive, affectionate, loyal, amusing, tolerant and playful and on occasion proud, calculating and stubborn, moreover they have a remarkable talent for survival as any soldier who has worked with them will vouchsafe.

What a character to give to the four-footed animal we know as the mule. What a better place the world would be if just a small percentage of humans could receive such an accolade.

A mule is the offspring of a female horse or pony and a male donkey. A female donkey mated with a mule horse or pony produces a hinny (sometimes known as a jennet). Mules can be of any size from around 17 hands (68in to the withers) down to 34in, and it is possible to breed whatever size and weight of mule needed by careful choice of parents.

Mules are generally infertile, although there have been, over the centuries, a few reports of supposedly fertile mules, and the Mule Society has been involved in the verification of several recent cases, in China and the USA, which have caused great interest in the scientific world.

Physically stronger than either parent, mules are sure-footed, longer-lived, have more stamina, can withstand extremes of climate better, are less prone to disease and more economical.

A mule can do anything a horse or donkey can do – and in many cases can do it better. Mules are perhaps best known for their virtues as pack animals, carrying everything from the famous 'screw-guns' on India's rugged Northwest Frontier, to building materials for the repair of a dam in the mountains of California.

As riding animals, mules have an exceptionally smooth gait, and their sure-footedness and stamina make them ideal for a wide variety of uses. In the USA they have become more and more popular over the last twenty years and compete against horses in many events, having been banned from taking part in some because they were considered 'unfair competition' – they kept winning!

Farm work was probably the mule's first task about 3,000 years ago, and in many parts of the world they still provide the only motive power on farms. The Roman public transport system made extensive use of mules, and they have been valued for driving ever since, perhaps most dramatically in recent times pulling the pioneers' wagons across America.

Hambone a mule attached to the United States Army died at Fort Carson, Colorado. He was quite a celebrity and had served much of his thirty-nine years with the Army. He received a full military funeral.

Most mules in Britain are fairly small, and are best suited to driving, pack work or as mounts for children, but due largely to encouragement by the British Mule Society, there are now several large jack donkeys in Britain which are available for the breeding of large mules. We look forward to seeing more and more large mules competing on equal terms with horses.

Yet the mule has never been looked upon with the same adoration which we give our horses and donkeys, yet more and more people are coming to realise what a superb animal it is in all manner of competitive events. This resurgence of interest is again due to the work of the British Mule Society.

The British Mule Society aims to encourage people to use mules, giving information and advice on breeding, purchase, training, welfare, care and management and any other aspect of mules.

— ∞ — ∞ — ∞ — ∞ — ∞ —

A Seal Sanctuary

— ∞ — ∞ — ∞ — ∞ — ∞ —

THE Seal Sanctuary at Gweek, Cornwall, is deservedly a great attraction to visitors and since a quite accidental start in 1957 is now making its name and work known all over the country and even abroad.

It all happened when Mr Ken Jones a miner in the Rhondda Valley threw up his job and moved to St Agnes, purchasing a small cafe. It was in the bay there one day, that his attention was drawn to a crowd on the beach watching a baby seal. She was a creamy white furry bundle, 3ft long and weighing about 30lb. Her umbilical cord was newly cut which indicated she was only a day or two old. They were later to realise that this was a regular occurrence when the pups get separated from their mothers and are being dashed against the rocks by heavy seas. Furthermore they cannot of course feed themselves and consequently die of malnutrition.

At first, attempts were made to push this youngster back into the sea, particularly as she was showing distress at the people and the barking dogs.

After several attempts the pup still came back to the beach and finally Mr and Mrs Jones decided to rescue it and carry it up to the bungalow for safety.

Having no knowledge of seals, they thought it should be kept in water and visitors lent a hand to fill a bath in which the baby was deposited. Various organisations were then phoned for advice and the consensus of opinion seemed to be, to put the pup back in the sea at Seal Cove, the seal's breeding ground. A boat was obtained and the seal put into the sea, but she kept coming back. Finally she swam off to the beach where they were unable to resist the pleading look in her eyes, so carried her up to a caravan. The next thing was to feed her and again they had no knowledge whatsoever. Again they phoned round and were told to try 12oz of margarine to 1pt of milk four times a day, but she would need force feeding by a tube into the pup's stomach. It was difficult to open her mouth and when this was achieved no milk went down for the pup had her teeth clenched on the tube. Despite all efforts she died, though the lessons learnt were put to good use in the future.

Due to this incident, as the days went by, people rang Mr Jones directly they saw a seal or anything else in the animal or bird world in trouble and so it all began. In due course the rescue service became a full time occupation and a move was made to Gweek and a purpose-built sanctuary was built to care for seals which were in trouble (see picture on back of jacket). A wealth of experience has been built up but the physical tasks of getting the seals up cliff paths and giving them medical attention did not decrease. The early experiences showed that trust and patience was the cornerstone in treating them, and each seal was an individual and often quite a character. As in humans, so there is always a clown, or a show-off. Others delight in amusing the public with tricks but there are also those who are timid and shy. They are also intelligent.

After a short while each new arrival recognises Mr Jones and greets him with enthusiasm much as a dog would.

Some seals with horrendous injuries are rescued and sad to say some of the wounds are caused by so-called humans. One, named Nelson, had been stoned by youngsters on the beach and lost an eye, part of a flipper and had ulcers all over its body. Such cases, apart from doctoring, took much care in patience to feed.

The winter of 1969-70 was a disastrous one. Malnutrition, septicaemia (a form of blood poisoning) and congestion of the lungs are very common, all of which can be treated if taken in time. Calls came in from all over Cornwall of seals rescued and they had to be fetched and treated. This particular winter there were at least fifty pups rescued, and virtually a whole generation of pups were wiped out with the atrocious weather. Some responded to treatment and when fully recovered were put back to sea.

One seal, Simon, had a wonderful temperament and was a real show-off who would do his own tricks to amuse the visitors. One such trick was to wind a hose pipe around himself and with this supporting his body would go to sleep. When Mr Jones was away for a few days he reacted as so many cats and dogs do, by sulking and ignoring the boss when he did come back. Like children, they need constant attention.

The sanctuary at Gweek today is a triumph of one man's love and dedication to these lovely creatures. There are now several pools separating the various groups. Weaning etc plus a fully equipped seal hospital. Each year thousands of visitors come as close as they ever will to watch these glorious and intelligent mammals.

The awful butchery that goes on annually in Canada, where 180,000 seal pups are clubbed to death just for the value of their skins to make wearing apparel for those who can afford it.

Heaven knows these babies suffer enough injuries at sea – starvation, seagull attacks, pollution – without man's vicious killings. It makes one wonder what sort of people can club and skin alive these youngsters with pleading eyes. Over fifty per cent of seal pups die naturally each year – before the age of six weeks.

A recent incident was when a baby seal was washed up on Fleet Beach, near Blackpool, with a broken back flipper. The local zoo would not accept it so two animal lovers who knew of the work of the sanctuary borrowed a special container and drove 400 miles through the night to Gweek.

The five-week-old baby was duly handed over and after a cup of tea they set off on their return journey. They said they were fully recompensed by seeing their patient put in the pool with all the other seals. The baby on a special diet, recovered in six weeks.

— ∞ — ∞ — ∞ — ∞ — ∞ —

In July 1988 a dreaded and completely unknown disease killed 7,000 seals in the North Sea, off the coast of England.

Experts from the Sea Mammal Research Station are divided over the precise cause of the epidemic, and whether it is due to a virus or pollution or both. Two suspect viruses have been found in dead and sick seals.

Britain's seal population is reckoned at 25,000 – half the European total, 6,000 of which are in and around the Wash.

It is for these reasons alone we should be grateful to Mr Jones, for he is bringing people face to face with this beautiful breed. Let us hope that so many people all over the world will rise and say 'no' to the selfish slaughter before seals join so many of nature's wonderful animals and become extinct.

— ∞ — ∞ — ∞ — ∞ — ∞ —

Help for the Disabled

— ∞ — ∞ — ∞ — ∞ — ∞ —

THE close relationship between owners and dogs for blind people is very well known to us. To see the dogs, conscious of their responsibility, taking their charges through busy streets and across roads is a joy.

Mrs Frances Hay of Leamington is disabled having had a half thigh amputation on her left leg when she was fifteen due to cancer of the bone. Such an affliction is usually fatal and it is a miracle that after some twenty years she is still alive and had as good a chance of surviving as anyone else.

Wearing an artificial leg, submits the good limb to considerable strain, causing the onset of arthritis. The disability makes it difficult in rising from a chair, mounting stairs and walking on uneven ground, and crossing roads, etc.

Mrs Hay needed a companion and went to the kennels for unwanted dogs, where she found Kim, a jet black Belgian Shepherd bitch – a beautiful animal which unfortunately suffered from chronic pancreas and digestive troubles. Due to this she had been taken to a home for unwanted dogs by her previous owners.

One look at her and despite her medical history Mrs Hay took her home.

In a very short while both dog and human found they had so much to give each other. The human cossetted the dog which responded by using its intelligence to help.

Whenever Mrs Hay was in difficulty she found Kim by her side and almost without thinking she would grasp Kim's neck or even her tail and steady herself.

It started quite spontaneously without any word of command and very quickly a complete affability grew up between them. Eventually she learned to come to assistance on command. The call, 'come and help me Kim' brought her scampering from wherever she happened to be.

For eight years Kim lived on to repay the kindness she had experienced for she seemed to know she was a burden and when she died it was a crushing blow to her owner.

It was this bond between them that first gave Mrs Hay the idea of starting a scheme for helping the disabled, for if she could be helped so obviously could many others in a variety of ways.

Mrs Hay's next dog was Amber, a German Shepherd bitch who followed Kim in becoming a demonstration dog. She turned out to be almost an identical replica in character, habits and personality.

From then on the work of founding an association of dogs for the disabled became a reality.

This was in October of 1986 since when Frances Hay and her organisation have achieved many notable successes in their attempts to present fully-trained dogs to worthy recipients. Amongst the dogs that have and are being successfully trained and donated are:-

Holly, the first companion dog to be presented by the Organisation, was a terrier cross. Holly was donated to the residents of a retirement home in Kenilworth where she has proved to be of enormous therapeutic value to all those around her.

Rani, a German Shepherd dog, was originally found wandering the streets of Coventry. She was trained to become the first fully-trained working dog by the Organisation, and was presented during August of 1987 to a disabled pensioner in Rugby.

Misty, found on the streets of Birmingham literally at death's door, now works primarily as a demonstration dog for the Organisation. Misty is a husky cross and accompanied Mrs Hay on all her visits to schools, dog shows and so forth to not only illustrate the role of the companion dog, but also to enable children and others to meet the Organisation dogs at first hand.

Poppy was the victim of a car accident. A collie/King Charles spaniel cross, Poppy was rescued and trained to become a most endearing companion/working dog. All that remains is to place the dog with a suitable recipient. Poppy's further training will depend very much on the particular disability of the future owner.

Sheena was another rescued from the kennels. Little is known about the background of this charming terrier/collie cross. Chosen for her remarkably gentle temperament, Sheena has also been trained to the standards demanded by the Organisation and is now awaiting a suitable recipient.

Companies and other organisations are coming forward with offers of assistance, financial and otherwise, for Dogs for the Disabled. As this support and encouragement increases, Frances Hay and her demonstration dogs continue to appear regularly at dog shows and conventions, offering everybody the opportunity to learn at first hand about dogs and their potential for the disabled.

Another example of the affinity between man and dog was that of a disabled lady who required a dog, mainly for companionship, as after her children and husband had left the home in the morning, she was alone all day. She suffered from quite severe disability – being paralysed down her left side, with very little speech and some impairment of vision. Thus they had to find a small, gentle, lightly coloured dog (because of the vision problem). It was achieved, and the lady came to the rescue kennels where they had found the dog to meet it and approve. Her husband took her to an open space in her wheelchair and the dog was duly brought to her. The dog very gently went up to the lady, put her front paws on her lap – with no prompting – and for the first time in nine years the lady moved her left arm to stroke the animal.

It is a cheering thought that not only were most of these dogs liable to be put down but having been rescued, they were able to become companions to disabled people thus adding a new dimension to the lives of both humans and animals.

The Dogs for the Disabled is still in its infancy but without any doubt will soon be known throughout the land.

[We regret to say that we learned of the death of Mrs Hay as the book went to press.]

Dogs for the Deaf

IN Great Britain one in five of the population has a significant hearing loss. Deaf people suffer isolation as well as social alienation; not only are they cut off from the sounds of conversation or music but also from the signals of danger, emergency and alarm.

During the past fifty years guide dogs for the blind have made a valuable contribution to the lives of blind people. Now new help is at hand for deaf people.

The Hearing Dogs for the Deaf scheme has been in operation since 1982, its aim is to train dogs to act as 'hearing ears' for deaf people by responding to everyday sounds, thus offering a realistic and practical means to greater independence. Since the scheme started a number of dogs have been successfully placed, proving their worth as hearing companions. With the continuing progress and expansion of the programme the training of many more dogs is planned.

Potential owners are carefully selected; they must be severely or profoundly deaf, with ability and desire to look after a dog properly. An experienced counsellor evaluates the application and is involved in familiarising the owner-to-be with their new hearing dog. A skilful dog trainer chooses a dog to suit the needs and wishes of that person. Dogs of high intelligence and friendly disposition, showing a keen response to sound and a willingness to please, are selected.

The dog is then trained to the sounds chosen by the new dog owner, such as a knock on the door, a whistling kettle, or the alarm clock. The dog can even be trained to fetch the deaf mother when her baby cries. A home-like environment is used for the training which is rigorous, but achieved by kindness and reward and takes about four months to complete. The counsellor is responsible for making pre and post placement visits to ensure that the dog and new owner are suited, happy and working well together.

A properly trained dog can give a deaf person a new feeling of independence, a practical means of 'hearing' certain sounds as well as the blessings of companionship and protection. In addition, the deaf person, having the responsibility of caring for the dog, can acquire greater awareness of the environment, which leads to a more fulfilling and satisfying life. Dogs are carefully selected from many sources: they may be offered by breeders or come from homes for stray dogs. In this way unwanted dogs can be trained to lead active and useful lives to the benefit of deaf people, in return for good appreciative homes.

The Hearing Dogs for the Deaf scheme receives no Government grant.

— ∞ — ∞ — ∞ — ∞ — ∞ —

A War Hero Remembered

— ∞ — ∞ — ∞ — ∞ — ∞ —

THE Royal Northumberland Fusiliers did not have an official mascot, but the story of Drummer the famous war dog of the Fighting Fifth is recalled for visitors to the Regiment's very fine museum at Alnwick Castle, Northumberland.

The handsome little fellow was born in 1893 and was the fifth of a litter of five. He accompanied his master, Capt G.S.L. Ray of the 5th Fusiliers, on service with the regiment in Egypt, Crete and South Africa.

This brave little animal's honours included the Queen's and Egyptian medals with clasps for Belmont, Modder River, Relief of Kimberley and other incidents. At Wyneberg he was wounded in the shoulder, and was present at many other engagements, snapping at flying bullets as if they were flies.

Drummer's master was killed at Maggersfontein but his comrades brought the faithful dog home to England to live with Captain Ray's father, the Principal Medical Officer at Colchester. It was in the hospital grounds there that this canine hero of a hundred fights met a sad and undignified death – poisoned by a bone that had been treated with strychnine. His death was recorded in *The Times* and many other national newspapers. Visitors to the Royal Northumberland Fusiliers Museum can see him today, a triumph of the taxidermist's art, as he was in life – a jaunty little terrier as fearless as the Fusiliers he served alongside for so many years.

— ∞ — ∞ — ∞ — ∞ — ∞ —

The Wild White Cattle

— ∞ — ∞ — ∞ — ∞ — ∞ —

THE story of Britain's herd of wild, white cattle provides a link with prehistoric times.

The cattle, reputed to be the most ferocious bovine species in the world, have grazed for centuries in the Park at Chillingham, near Alnwick, Northumberland, former estate of the Earls of Tankerville.

They are probably the last survivors of the savage herds which once roamed all over Britain; their origin is obscure, but they are thought to be descendants of the wild ox which inhabited northern Europe in prehistoric times. That species was said to be dark, the bulls being nearly black but with a white dorsal stripe. The Eighth Earl of Tankerville advanced the theory that possibly the Druids, by a process of segregation and selective slaughter, eventually managed to produce a white animal of the kind they highly prized for sacrificial purposes.

The present herd is unvaryingly true to type and no coloured or even partly coloured calf is ever born into it. The cattle have dark eyes, black muzzles and hoofs, fox-red hair inside the ears and black tips to their horns, when fully developed.

It seems fairly certain that herds of these wild cattle once roamed the Border forests which extended from Chillingham to the Clyde estuary. In the year 1250, a wall was built round the park at Chillingham and one of the herd was corralled, perhaps for food, perhaps for sport. When the Border reavers made their frequent raids, they were unable to drive away cattle as wild as these, so the herd remained and is still at Chillingham after 700 years. During all this time no extraneous blood has ever been introduced. Certainly the cattle have never been tamed and even today no human can approach them incorrectly without risk to his life.

A record of 1692 refers to 'my Lord's Beastes' but no number is given. In the last century there were between sixty and eighty. In 1925 there were about forty, but after the severe winter of 1947 the herd was threatened with extinction, reduced to eight cows and five bulls, all the younger beasts having perished. For eighteen months no calves were born, then a slow process of recovery began until by 1974 the size of the herd reached fifty animals which is considered to be the maximum number that the present acreage of the park can sustain.

Scientists and animal breeders are intrigued by the question of inbreeding, for the mating and breeding is left entirely to nature. The results are carefully watched, and the knowledge acquired may one day prove of great value to breeders of domestic cattle. No matter what the size of the herd, the sex proportion has been fairly constant in the ratio of three females to two males. Nature, by the principle of 'kinship', ensures that only the best blood is passed on to the next generation. Only the strongest and fittest bull becomes 'king', for to obtain the position he must defeat in combat any bull which challenges him. Inevitably the day comes when he in turn is beaten in battle, and then he is temporarily banished from the herd. He may come back and make another bid for leadership, but even if he is successful his new 'reign' will be short. Death in a fight is unusual but it does sometimes occur. From 1947-55 there was only one 'king' bull – quite a long reign. All the present animals are his progeny. They ruthlessly follow the savage law of nature, and a sick or wounded beast, knowing by instinct that it is an outcast, usually goes away from the herd of its own accord; if not, it is speedily ejected by its fellows.

A fascinating fact, that seems to be a throwback to ancient times, is that the animals have preserved their instinct about natural foes such as wolves. They ignore a shepherd's dog, but if a pack of foxhounds come into the park they immediately form themselves into a close group preparatory to stampeding. If the danger materialises and the hounds come really close, the herd stampedes in close formation with the cows in front, calves in the centre and the bulls at the rear, the 'king' bull taking up the rearguard station.

There is a resemblance between the Chillingham wild cattle and the Shorthorn and the Ayrshire. The bulls weigh about half a ton and the cows some 7cwt. Their weight and brawn, however, are deceptive, for in spite of their size one has been known to make a standing jump of 6ft.

This amazing breed lives on with little assistance from man beyond the provision of hay during the winter months and the removal of dead animals. For many years now they have been neither hunted nor shot. They retain their instinctive dislike of the scent of humans but at least they have become accustomed to the sight of man, provided he does not get too close. For man's part, the herd is of the greatest scientific and historical interest.

The cattle are now owned and maintained by a registered charity, the Chillingham Wild Cattle Association Limited. The public may go and see the herd whilst accompanied by the Park Warden, the park being open six days a week, (excepting Tuesdays) between 1 April and 31 October and on Bank Holidays. During the winter months the herd may be seen by appointment by parties of not less than four.

Proud Mascots of British Regiments

IT is an old saying that every dog has his day, but few if any have as many special days as Melantor Connor, the Irish wolfhound mascot of the Irish Guards. He has the privilege of meeting members of the Royal Family and is often present on occasions of pageantry.

He has a touch of royalty about him too, for he is named after a king of Ulster who reigned some 2,000 years ago.

Connor was presented to the Irish Guards in February 1985 by Miss Margaret Harrison, who also presented the previous mascot, Cormac of Tara, to the regiment.

Connor lives with his handler, L/Sgt David Rutherford and his family, and started his training at the age of six months when he was introduced to the Band of the Irish Guards who played soft music at their first introduction before building up to louder music after a few days. His next hurdle was to get used to the band playing behind him as he marched.

In his time as mascot, he has met most of the Royal Family and appeared several times on television, notably on *Blue Peter*. He also took part in the wedding of the Duke and Duchess of York, and every St Patrick's Day Connor gets presented with a spray of shamrock by Her Majesty Queen Elizabeth, The Queen Mother.

As part of his duties, the mascot spends at least three weeks each year in Northern Ireland where he is a popular attraction and a very good recruiting feature. He has settled into the life of a working dog, mounting guard at

Buckingham Palace and Windsor Castle regularly.

As befits his status Connor has a considerable wardrobe, including two coats of red Irish linen and one of grey. He also has a grey sheepskin for use in very cold weather. He has two collars, that used for State occasions is of solid silver. The other is made of leather, on which is inscribed his name along with two Staff Cap Stars, which is worn each time that he does a public duty.

The first mascot of the Regiment was Brian Boru who served from 1900-10 and was succeeded by seven others, whose service averaged six to seven years.

There are several other mascots serving with regiments:

The Royal Regiment of Fusiliers	Indian black buck
The Royal Welch Fusiliers	Goat
The Royal Irish Rangers	Wolfhound
The Worcestershire and	
Sherwood Foresters Regiment	Ram
The Argyll and Sutherland Highlanders	Shetland Pony
The Parachute Regiment	Shetland Pony

— ∞ — ∞ — ∞ — ∞ — ∞ —

The Battersea Dogs' Home

— ∞ — ∞ — ∞ — ∞ — ∞ —

AS he hears a different step, the little black-and-tan mongrel perks up. Rising on his hind legs, his front paws scratching at the bars, tail wagging furiously, he sniffs frantically with anticipation and hope. Can it possibly be someone coming for him? In seconds it is all over, he slinks back to curl up miserably as he has done a hundred times before – a picture of utter dejection. This isn't his master or mistress; once again he must give up hope. This is something that happens every day to most of the animals in the greatest dogs' home in the world – at Battersea, London.

Every week about 200 dogs are collected from police stations all over London, where they have been taken as strays. Some are in fine fettle and are obviously genuinely lost. Most were once eagerly adopted pets. Some have been attached to the same family for years; others were purchased with great enthusiasm but, after a few days or weeks, when the novelty had worn off were discarded as a nuisance. In the holiday season particularly, a large number are deliberately 'lost' so that their owners do not have to take them with them or pay to have them boarded.

The mind of a dog lover boggles at the mentality of a human who can have a dog for years and then, when it grows 'too large', becomes old or dirty, or is about to have pups, can take it to some deserted spot and make off, leaving it well behind.

But these are the less tragic cases which occur every day at the home. Some of the dogs are really ill when they are brought in and have to be destroyed. This, too, is the fate of most of the puppies under six months, which have not been inoculated against distemper and hard-pad. Every day each week (except Sunday) five ambulances tour the Greater London area calling at 189 police stations. Almost every station will have one or more strays waiting. Some will be starving, though if they have been at a police station for even a few hours, the edge will have been taken off their appetite by the kindly arm of the law. The dogs are taken to Battersea, checked for health, and then kept for a minimum of seven days in the hope that the owners will call and collect them.

It is a pity that the people who 'lose' their dogs cannot see the creatures' reactions when the ambulance brings them to Battersea after a round of calls. As the van pulls up inside the yard and the doors are thrown open, the smells of a whole new world strike the dogs inside. Bewildered, they sit there without excitement, without the tail wagging one associates with any new experience for a dog and without the eager inquisitiveness. They make little effort to get out. Occasionally one of the load will bound forward and lick the attendant, as if he has been lost for a long time and yearns for company, any company. The majority just sit in the van and look a little hurt, yet dignified, as most animals do outside a circus or a zoo.

In an average year about seventeen per cent of the dogs brought in are claimed by their owners; some forty per cent, most of which are sick or of bad temperament, are destroyed; forty-three per cent are sold after the seventh day, and immense care is taken to see that these go to good homes and do not end up victims of the vivisection trade or in homes where they will be a nine-day wonder.

The total number of animals dealt with is amazing. In an average year it amounts to between 17,000–20,000 mostly collected from police stations; yet the number of dogs reported lost every year is a little in excess of 5,000. The number of stray dogs in the London area has mounted by about 1,000 a year over the last fifteen years. Those who deal with them give a variety of reasons for this. One of the primary reasons would seem to be the movement of people in the London area into flats or different houses. Very frequently a condition of the letting is that 'no animals are allowed' and, whereas a few owners faced with this will take their pet to a home where perhaps another owner can be found for it, the majority just dump or lose them.

There is a growing feeling that far fewer dogs would be adopted light heartedly as pets without consideration for the time and trouble involved in keeping and exercising them, if a dog registration scheme was introduced.

The case history of many of the individual dogs arriving at the Home can be pathetic indeed. There was, for instance, a poodle in fine condition, found with a note written by two children tucked inside his collar. The note explained, in heart-broken terms, that the parents had been on a housing list for a very long time and had at last been offered accommodation – with the rule 'no pets'. So Kim was eventually taken to

Battersea Dogs' Home. A few days later, however, a tearful family collected him. They found they missed him so much that they were prepared to forgo the offer of new and better housing conditions. There was a happier ending than most to this episode, for the story appeared in the press and someone was so touched by the family's loyalty that they offered a house where Kim could go too.

Another case involved a Nottingham lorry driver, who called at Battersea in the hope of finding his boon companion, a labrador, who had jumped from his cab at a busy crossing in London. It was impossible for him to stop at the time and when he could there was no trace of the dog. Some days later, however, the dog duly arrived at the Home. The owner was notified, and picked up his pet on the next trip south.

A crane operator, working on the side of the Thames one day, saw a dog struggling in the water. He made several attempts to rescue it and at last did so, only to find that the poor thing was starving, its ribs jutting through its coat. He took it home and surreptitiously gave the stray the dinner which had been prepared for himself. His wife persuaded him to take the dog to the police station. Not very willingly he did so, and then got into his car and drove off. When he stopped at the traffic lights farther down the road, he saw the dog he had just left crossing the road in a frantic effort to get to his car. After that there was only one thing for it; formalities completed, the dog was his, and they are today inseparable.

Perhaps one of the most heart-rending cases, while it lasted, was that of the seven-year-old lad who called at Battersea to report the loss of his mongrel. 'You see,' he told the officials with the seriousness of a child, 'he suffers from kidney trouble and he will be very ill without me.' For fourteen days the child called daily and, as his unhappiness was making him ill, his parents too searched high and low for the lost animal. The child's visits to the Home were punctuated with new brainwaves thought up in his desperation. One day he brought a photograph to make sure the officials would recognise the dog when they saw him. The next he reported he had left a light burning in the window all night so that, if his dog saw it, he would know it was his house. Rarely have the staff, who certainly have some pathetic cases to deal with, felt so desperately sorry; but when seven weeks had passed, all but the child had given up hope. Then the miracle happened. A dog answering to the description was brought in. It was the right one, and there was not a dry eye among those who witnessed the reunion between the dog and his young master.

Examples such as these go some way to compensate for the shocking cruelty and neglect which so many of the dogs have met. Some have been wandering for weeks in a starving condition, some are so ill that they can hardly drag themselves along. Among recent cases of bitches turned out by their owners when about to whelp was a small dog who, having given birth to six tiny puppies, stood guard over them so ferociously that even to feed her needed the utmost caution.

Very often the seven-day rule is not strictly adhered to. One man used to bring his dog in whenever the law caught up with him and he received a prison sentence. This was all right until he was given a really long stretch. Even then the Home carried on, and when at last the man was released his first call was to collect his dog.

One section of the kennels at Battersea is a sad place, for it houses the animals destined to be put down painlessly. Perhaps they have been brought in injured, terribly maltreated or just too sick. There is nothing else for it; they have to die, and anyone looking at them can see that they sense it. Labradors, spaniels, dobermans, mongrels, whippets, alsatians, greyhounds – almost every known breed or intermediate breed of dog arrives at some time or another.

This, of course, is one of the puzzles. One can begin to understand a small mongrel dog not being claimed, but how can one explain a St Bernard or a Great Dane being missing and no one enquiring after it? These large animals are often brought in by the ambulances and obviously do not come from the East End, which perhaps is responsible for the largest number of strays. Fashion in dogs changes from time to time and this makes a difference to the activities in the Dogs' Home. Until 1961, for instance, a poodle was a rarity; now the Home handles quite a number.

The Home traditionally carries three canine residents, and usually they are real characters. One such was Tina. When BOAC was experimenting with a new container for use in jet planes, a request was made for a dog to go on a trial trip, and Tina was lent. She flew to Prestwick and back, and acquitted herself very well indeed.

Somewhere in the region of a hundred people a day visit the Home. Some are hoping to find their lost pet, others go to buy one. The way the preconceived ideas of this latter group change before they have been in the place many minutes is remarkable. They arrive feeling quite certain just what they want and spend a long time describing their particular requirements. Then, as they go round, they are unable to withstand the wistful look of one dog, or the pathetic eagerness of another. Generally all their firm resolves melt, and they go off thrilled and triumphant with the last kind of dog they ever expected to possess.

This great Home was founded at Holloway in 1860 by a Mrs Tealby. Her purpose was to give succour and shelter to the waifs and strays of London's dog world and the very idea was greeted with derision and ridicule. Within three years, however, 35,000 dogs were being dealt with annually within a twelve mile radius of Charing Cross. In 1896, a rabies scare took the number up to 42,000. The home was removed to its present site in 1871. The work has never been government subsidised and is financed purely by public subscription. The premises have now been partially rebuilt and thoroughly modernised. The kennels have under-floor heating, infra-red lighting and fibreglass beds. A staff of thirty-four works under the direction of the secretary.

In addition to dogs, much is done for cats, nearly 1,000 of

these being handled each year. No animal is ever turned away. A fox captured at Canvey Island was given shelter until the RAF unit at Binbrook adopted him as their mascot. From time to time rabbits, and even monkeys turn up.

There is a large out-patients' department at Battersea, where the pets of old-age pensioners and children are dealt with, some 700 animals paying visits each year.

As a tribute to the foundress, the following verse by Byron appears each year in the annual report of the Dogs' Home:

With eye upraised, his master's look to scan,
The joy, the solace, and the aid of man;
The rich man's guardian and the poor man's friend,
The only creature faithful to the end.

— ∞ — ∞ — ∞ — ∞ — ∞ —

A Unique Swannery

— ∞ — ∞ — ∞ — ∞ — ∞ —

NEARLY a thousand years ago King Canute of England reigned (1016-1035), and it was his major domo who created a swannery on the Dorsetshire coast, run by the monks of the nearby Abbey.

In those days swans were a much prized item of food. Today the whole estate still flourishes, particularly the swannery which in those days contained some 400 swans. It is now the only managed swannery in the world. No visitor to Dorset or indeed further afield should miss going to see it.

Conservation is today all the rage but this swannery is a prime example of what has been going on in this field for centuries and gives an insight into the wonder and beauty of wildlife.

It is a wonderful experience for visitors to see these birds at close quarters, surely the most majestic and beautiful of any British species. Here they are free to come and go, free to feed in the lush feeding grounds, free to nest and bring up their young and live in idyllic surroundings. None of them are ever pinioned or clipped. There are not just dozens but there can be up to 500 of them. In the winter season this figure has been known to rise to 1,200.

The swannery is one of the great sights of the British countryside.

The birds come from a wide area for the food which is to be found here in the 'Fleet', an area of water lying snugly behind the famous Chesil Beach on the Dorset coast. Except for a narrow outlet at one end, this natural lagoon is to all intents and purposes a place of peace and lush feeding. The whole swannery area however, stretches for eight miles along the Chesil Beach.

Whilst many swans have taken up permanent residence other birds mostly come from the Somerset Levels and the Devon rivers, Exe, Axe and Otter. Some come from farther afield. They all know where they can find an inexhaustible and favourite nutritious food – eel grass, which covers the bed of the 'Fleet'. In February they come to nest. They mate in the water and then come to the meadows beyond, to build their nests. Despite some fifty pairs nesting at the same time, there is little trouble for they do not seem to mind near neighbours. The late arrivals, however, may find it difficult to find a site for their nests and even build on the pathways. They are quite used to humans and in May visitors may walk between them, the birds being quite unconcerned.

Their nests, made of the ample available reed and grass are quite large, varying between 2ft and 7ft across and usually some inches to 3ft above ground. The usual clutch of eggs is six and the Pen (female) lays them at two day intervals and does not sit on them for incubation until the last is laid and this one, by reason of not being allowed to get cold, often does not hatch or is a weakling. It is odd that it all seems quite haphazard inasmuch as the Wardens can remove two or three eggs and replace them with man-made substitutes, this being done to fool the fox.

Devotedly protective when the cygnets are young, the birds seem quite unconcerned when they are first born. Usually swans mate for life and each pair have their own area of territory. As a result fights break out, but much of the time it is ritualised posturing. Battles ensue and on rare occasions the Cob (male) will fight. With the strength of their wings they could possibly break a man's arm or leg, but generally the vanquished dies from drowning after wounds and sheer exhaustion.

The eggs take thirty-five days to hatch and the cygnets take some time to learn the call of their parents. For this reason some of the families are penned for a short period. The birds are majestic and when fully grown a very large male can weigh up to 40lb. The cygnets reach maturity after three to four years.

In addition, some 2,000 coots abound in the reserve and here and there are other visitors such as a flamingo who has been there so long that it is accepted as a swan. There are also very occasionally a few black swans and an abundance of rare wild fowl. Wild duck are also very numerous and the visitor may see the decoys and traps built so that certain of them may be ringed for scientific records which began in 1930. No longer are these birds decoyed to be shot for food.

There is a heronry close by which has been occupied for centuries.

The staff are absolutely dedicated and consist of a Swanherd, a Deputy Swanherd, a Fleet Warden, a Wildlife officer and Herdsman and an Education Officer, part of whose duties is to lecture to schools and other organisations.

The whole area is an excellent example of what conservation and care of wildlife is all about.

The birds are fed three times a day, and they do not have to be very old to find the time and place where that takes place.

This is a paradise for bird lovers and photographers. It is

also an ideal place to take children to see wildlife at its best for there are walks round the complex and even a hide.

Swans are an example to the human race, for they lead an exemplary family life. The family keep together until it is time for the cygnets to make their own way, and of course there is no question of divorce among the parents during the mating period. The average life of a swan can be in excess of ten years. At the age of four the young ones are ready to breed.

Every community has its 'tough guy' and one swan who was born at the swannery some fourteen years ago is a case in point. Though by no means one of the largest, he guards the stretch of water which is his territory year after year very fiercely, and woe betide anything that comes too near for he can be quite ferocious.

There are a few predators. Sometimes a very clever fox may take a cygnet and Greater Blackback gulls take many cygnets but the cob and pen are very protective of their family. The cob particularly will fight to the death giving the pen and cygnets time to escape.

A rather interesting sideline is that at moulting time the feathers are collected and made into quill pens for Lloyds of London who by tradition use them for recording in their 'Doom' book of ships lost at sea.

— ∞ — ∞ — ∞ — ∞ — ∞ —

A Sanctuary for Donkeys

— ∞ — ∞ — ∞ — ∞ — ∞ —

WITHOUT doubt, the much abused and humble animal, the donkey, is the most lovable, docile creature the good Lord put in to the animal kingdom. Moreover a great help to humans especially in poorer countries. It is therefore quite incomprehensible that they seem to suffer the most neglect and cruelty of any four-legged beast.

How the idea ever came about to equate stupidity to donkeys when there are so many humans around defeats me.

In Britain it is bad enough but in some other lands the cruelty is beyond belief and in a wide spectrum. As always, there are champions and once having dealt with donkeys, they get a fantastic hold on those who begin to understand them.

Such a case is that of Mrs E Svendsen whose introduction to them was a pet for her children and gradually her work for the sick, overworked and cruelly treated of the species, became a life's work. From the first donkey in 1961 her work has become famous at home and abroad, and today she is responsible for the care of well in excess of 3,000. The story of the work already well documented nevertheless bears some repetition.

The Donkey Sanctuary, near Sidmouth, Devon, founded in 1969 is now the sixty-fourth largest charity in Britain and is now contained in five farms including the Slade Handicapped Centre.

The turning point to the venture occurred when Mrs Svendsen went to Exeter Market out of curiosity and saw seven terrified donkeys in a cramped pen. They were in terrible condition and full of lice and the ruffians who were handling them seemed no better than sadists. Twisting the tails of the animals to hurry them on and beating them with sticks was common. When remonstrated, the typical reply, 'These buggers just want a clout'. The seven donkeys were purchased and from then on, the work of rescue went ahead.

It is amazing that in a nation of animal lovers so much cruelty can be inflicted on animals, particularly those with such a gentle and kindly disposition, though it must be said that much stems from ignorance.

Donkeys began to arrive at the Sanctuary in terrible condition. Some were walking skeletons, others full of lice and covered in sores.

One rescue was of a terribly bad case where the poor animal had been working on a car dump. She was covered in sores and her feet were cut to ribbons, caused by walking up and down on the piles of wrecked car metal. After her arrival at the Sanctuary she lay down for three weeks but with constant attention was brought back to health. She lived out her life happily for four years.

Another arrived covered in sores and with pieces of rotting sacking stuck to him. Some on arrival have galls into which a man could put his fist.

Mindless vandals had been at another and had nearly cut his ears off, while some half wits, had endeavoured to castrate another, using broken bottles as surgical instruments.

How men can treat these animals with such brutal and fiendish cruelty is beyond comprehension. It says a lot for the donkeys that after such treatment they still retain faith in humans.

The animals show much more compassion to each other. In a hot summer they will queue up patiently to take their turn in a dust bath. Cases have been known where donkeys have taken up station on each side of a blind one and gently nudged him away from obstacles. Abroad they have been known to cluster together to drive off wild dogs. At the Sanctuary the donkeys sense something wrong and frequently in the middle of the night will set up a collective bray.

As time went on and the charity grew, five different farms were acquired and no donkey has ever been turned away. Each animal has an individuality of its own. There is always a comedian or an extra inquisitive one, but they are all loveable creatures and their gentleness towards their fellows is a byword. This is not the only way they can teach humans a thing or two.

There are sometimes lighter moments, as when a donkey who had been used to a pint of beer each day was brought in. He made it quite clear by braying that he still needed it. First it was watered down then he was gradually weaned off it altogether.

People were shocked to read of the donkey victim selected for a Lent Fiesta in Villanueva de la Vera in Spain in 1987. Part of the so-called festival was, having selected a donkey, to place a thick collar round its neck and a rope with fifty knots in it attached to the collar.

The fattest man in the village was then masked and seated on the donkey, the villagers then took up position, each holding a knot, and the donkey was then dragged along the cobbled street. Each time it fell it was beaten until it could no longer rise when it was reputedly crushed to death.

Efforts were made by Mrs Svendsen the previous year to save the chosen donkey, but in 1987 the International Donkey Protection Trust made a point of stirring up public opinion in the hope that Blackie the 1987 chosen victim could be saved.

Mrs Svendsen spoke on radio and television to draw attention to the dastardly cruelty. The media was also alerted. It all paid off and though Blackie was used in the Fiesta he was allowed, due to public opinion, to escape final death. The *Star* newspaper and representatives from the Donkey Sanctuary purchased the donkey and after many trials and tribulations brought him home to the Sanctuary.

We hear talk of man's 'inhumanity to man', but the very thought of the poor defenceless, terrified animal being used to 'entertain' the villagers of Spain in such a way puts even bull-fighting in the shade.

Blackie received a wonderful welcome back at the Sanctuary and was very soon brought back to health and continues to live out his life now surrounded by love and comfort (see picture on the back of jacket).

Oblivious of the fact, Blackie, through Mrs Svendsen and the *Star* newspaper, has struck a blow for animal welfare, and emphasises the work of the new charity, the International Donkey Protection Trust.

Links are forged with many other societies and other countries including Ethiopia, Cyprus, South America, Middle East, Greece, North Africa, North America, Europe, Jamaica,

Turkey and Peru. Everywhere efforts are being made to introduce a code of practice, for example, the weight the animals carry and hours worked etc.

The magnitude of the work may be gauged from the fact that in Mexico alone there are six million donkeys.

At the Sidmouth Donkey Sanctuary the work goes on with ever far reaching results. There are two full-time vets always on hand and a well equipped hospital, for donkeys continually arrive from all parts of the country, many alas, showing atrocious neglect, but usually with love and care they are nurtured back to health. With careful treatment donkeys have a life span of fifty years.

In 1978 the Slade Centre for Handicapped Children was founded, at first with a few children enjoying the experience and today it provides endless pleasure for over 200 children. A special cart pulled of course by a donkey is in demand for those unable to sit on a donkey.

The donkeys each have a name, such as Naughty Face, Twiggy, Fuzzy, Gypo, Bill, Ben, Angelina, Peanuts, Pancho, Pinnochio, Treacle etc.

As Tiny Tim would have no doubt said, 'God Bless them everyone'.

The Donkey Sanctuary is open from 9am to 5pm, seven days a week, every month and there is no charge for admission.

In 1981 Mrs Svendsen was deservedly awarded the MBE for her work. She has written several books on the work of the Charity.

— ∞ — ∞ — ∞ — ∞ — ∞ —

Magnificent Animals

— ∞ — ∞ — ∞ — ∞ — ∞ —

THERE was rejoicing at Chester Zoo in 1989 when their three-year-old Siberian Tiger Natasha gave birth to twin cubs. The first tiger cubs to be born at the zoo for ten years, they were magnificent offspring and subsequently named Korda (the male) and Strelka (female) and like most of the young animals, particularly the cat family, were adorable. They were of course cuddly kittens but now at twelve months are almost fully grown and very lively.

The mother remained in her den with them until they were nearly six weeks old, and then one morning picked the youngsters up one at a time and proudly took them outside to be admired by visitors.

During that six weeks the mother was not disturbed at all for any interference might have caused the mother to abandon or even kill the youngsters.

The parents of these two youngsters are majestic specimens and weigh anything between 400–600lb. Their feeding consists of some 15lb of beef on the bone plus an addition of mineral supplement for five days a week. They have two rest days from eating – an example that so many humans might follow!

Now Korda and Strelka weigh something between 500/600lb and are a very handsome pair.

Siberian Tigers (*Panthera Tigris Altaica*) come from the western side of the USSR and are one of the rarest of the remaining five sub species found from India through S E Asia into China and Russia.

It is now listed as an endangered species.

— ∞ — ∞ — ∞ — ∞ — ∞ —

One of the young chicks currently being reared in the incubation house at the zoo is growing very rapidly, and will eventually have a wingspan of over 8ft.

She is an Andean Condor, the first hatched at the zoo for two years. Chester is the only British zoo breeding condors.

The young chick is being hand-reared, because it was feared that she may not survive if left with the parent birds. The bird staff were anxious that the chick should not become imprinted on its keeper, and as the education department have recently become very adept at puppet making their help was enlisted. A condor glove puppet was designed, but some difficulty was experienced in getting the beak to act realistically. The zoo's blacksmith put in some work on a bull-dog clip and eventually an art teacher at a County High School completed the job from moulded plastic. The puppet body, made from specially dyed fabric, was the final touch. Two puppets were made – a male and a female!

The chick is happily feeding from her puppet parents. It would take some imagination to call her beautiful and her eating habits aren't exactly dainty, but she's a great achievement for the dedication of the bird staff.

Legislation of Dangerous Dogs

$- \infty - \infty - \infty - \infty - \infty -$

IN 1991, following a spate of attacks by dangerous dogs on humans, Parliament rushed through special legislation. The Dangerous Dogs Act came into force, just thirty-three days following its introduction. It became a criminal offence to keep a designated fighting dog in public without a muzzle and a leash. Initially the restrictions applied to four breeds – the American pit bull terrier, the Japanese Tosa, the Fila Braziliera and the Dogo Argentino – although under the new law the Home Secretary had reserve powers to impose restrictions on any other breed if necessary.

From 12 August 1991 the owners of the estimated 10,000 fighting dogs in Britain were prevented from exchanging, trading, breeding or giving away their pets, and forbidden to advertise them for sale.

It will also be considered an offence to allow them to stray or wander. Failure to comply with any of the new rules carries a penalty after conviction of a £2,000 fine and/or six months' imprisonment.

Wildlife in London

WILDLIFE does not just exist in the countryside. Many species have adapted themselves to city life. Hedgehogs, toads, owls, foxes, kestrels and plants of all kinds can live alongside people.

Wherever there is an open space in London, plants and animals are to be found and the London Wildlife Trust exists to protect them.

The Trust was established in 1981 and is now the country's leading urban wildlife group. They have set up over thirty wildlife sites throughout the Greater London area, where plants and animals are protected. They want people to be more aware of the wildlife all around them, and wherever possible their nature reserves are open to the public and schoolchildren.

The Trust has conducted a series of successful surveys of London's wildlife, notably Fox Watch and Owl Prowl. Foxes and other animals and birds are more common than one might think – more than 2,000 people reported seeing foxes in less than two weeks!

One of the strangest animals to be captured in the back garden of a council housing estate in Stoke Newington, London, was a Muntjak, a tiny female deer, smaller than the average deer.

The Muntjak is originally a native of China and India but is thought to have established itself after escaping from private collections.

They are shy little animals, very strong and can travel very fast. The body of a similar animal was discovered a year or so

197

ago near Hampstead Heath, which now give rise to specula-
tion that the animals may be living and multiplying near the
Heath. The recent find is now sharing an enclosure in a park
with some tame fallow deer.

Conservation of wildlife areas requires constant management; members of the Trust carry out a variety of practical
tasks.

It has discovered some unusual and nationally rare plants
growing within London. Amongst the most interesting is the
narrow leaved water dropwart found in Hillingdon during
the extensive London Wildlife Habitat Survey. The last
record was made early in the nineteenth century.

There are some thirty-seven sites in the London area.

— ∞ — ∞ — ∞ — ∞ — ∞ —

New York Has 24,000,000 Cats

— ∞ — ∞ — ∞ — ∞ — ∞ —

THERE was an appalling story going the rounds of New
York not long ago. A newspaper report stated that
'...132 cats had been dropped seven storeys and ... only three
died.'

Pet lovers roused themselves to fury and wrote to the
Animal Medical Center in New York, demanding that such
cruelty be immediately stopped. The Center, equally horri-
fied, looked into the matter and the following were the facts:

Nobody deliberately dropped the cats as a part of a
medical experiment. The animals they saw and treated had
either jumped or accidentally fallen out of the windows in

high-rises and were brought to the Animal Medical Center for emergency treatment.

A resident at the treatment center decided to do a study on the cats – how far they fell, the nature of the injuries sustained and how many died. The results of this study were published in a veterinary journal.

The wire services and other media picked up the story. Unfortunately, the facts were garbled and misleading. This is an excellent example of how poor reporting can do an enormous amount of damage.

Which just goes to show that we cannot believe all we read in the newspapers.

The results of the study, by the Medical Centre, on the 132 cats that were brought in after falling from high-rise buildings was nevertheless amazing. One of the cats actually fell thirty-two storeys and walked away with only chest and lung bruises and a chipped tooth.

The cat's ability to land on its belly, not its feet, may explain why only three of the 132 felines that fell from great heights were dead on arrival at a veterinary hospital. The others recovered. About one-third were critically injured and required 'emergency life-sustaining treatment'. Another third required treatment for broken bones, bruises and cuts. A final third merely required observation in a hospital. The study shows a fallen cat's chances of survival are good.

The Animal Medical Center, Speyer Hospital and Caspary Research Institute of New York, founded in 1910, do an amazing job. Apart from treating some 64,000 animals a year, it also provides a teaching hospital. The total staff of nearly 300 people includes 70 vets.

We are indebted to the New York Center for the following items about cats.

The Center has an Exotic Animal clinic and the patients range from a macaw recovering from lead poisoning, a myna bird that flew into a wall, an iguana suffering malnutrition to a 50lb python suffering from a mouth infection. There was also the police dog 'Bandit' who had been injured while on the trail of three escaped convicts form Sing Sing prison.

Dog Data

Dogs have excellent hearing – they can hear some sounds at 80ft that people can't at 20ft.

Ancient Greeks believed that a person always accompanied by a dog would never suffer from insanity.

Fido comes from the Latin word 'fidus' meaning faithful or trustworthy.

The first space traveller was a Russian dog, 'Laika', who made his journey in 1957.

A one-year-old dog has about the same maturity level as a 16-year-old person.

It's illegal for a dog to chase a cat up a telephone pole in International Falls, Minnesota. Owners can be arrested and fined.

Cat Data

Cats are 'digitigrade' animals – they run on their toes with their heels up.

Cats have a third eyelid called a nictitating membrane. Unlike their regular eyelids, it closes on an angle to provide more eye protection.

Cats, like dogs, must be vaccinated every year against rabies. In fact, feline rabies in the US has nearly tripled in the last five years.

Purring doesn't originate in a cat's throat – it begins in the blood system. The actual sound results from the vibrations of blood vessels in the cat's chest. All cats purr, but some do it so softly it can't be heard. The vibration can be felt by touching the cat's throat.

A cat can see objects in very little light, things that the human eye can't perceive. But cats can't see if there's no light all.

Cats seem to have an excellent memory. Even after long separations, they remember their former owners. And, of course, we know they remember a trip to the vet.

The average healthy adult cat sleeps about sixty-five per cent of the time.

According to the Center there are 36,000,000 dog owning households and 24,000,000 cat owning households in the United States.

— ∞ — ∞ — ∞ — ∞ — ∞ —

At Home and Abroad

— ∞ — ∞ — ∞ — ∞ — ∞ —

A 150lb grey-rumped hog may well be grunting with satisfaction. Together with a German Shepherd dog, Calamity Bob, they have been left a share in a £350,000 estate left by an American lady from Iowa who died in 1990.

— ∞ — ∞ — ∞ — ∞ — ∞ —

An even stranger case was the bequest of £26,000 left by a spinster to her thirty-four-year-old tortoise. The will expressed the money should be used 'for the care, maintenance and upkeep of her pet for the rest of its natural life'. The lady's nearest relative received only £350 and a few family photographs. As a tortoise lives to an average of seventy years, at the height of luxurious living the chelonian will live well on lettuce and courgettes.

— ∞ — ∞ — ∞ — ∞ — ∞ —

The Giant Panda, 18-year-old Chia-Chia, was sent from London Zoo to Mexico City Zoo in 1988 to meet his mate, Tohui, once described as the Sophia Loren of the panda world and zoological world. It was hoped there would be a successful mating as a result of the union. Two years later a birth occurred (July 1990) to the delight of London Zoo officials. This latest cub is only the eighth to be born in Mexico Zoo.

— ∞ — ∞ — ∞ — ∞ — ∞ —

Strange to say pigs are becoming the fashionable pets in the United States. The favourite is the Vietnamese pot bellied strain.

The pig is a much maligned animal for it is simply not true that they are dirty animals. They are naturally very clean which is more than can be said for the conditions in which the majority are kept.

The smallest pig is the 'Mini Malaline'. The piglet weighs about the same as a tin of beans.

The largest pig on record was a hog which weighed over 2,000lb.

— ∞ — ∞ — ∞ — ∞ — ∞ —

An exotic bird dealer took over from an incubator when New York, where she lives, suffered a severe power cut.

She took the clutch of 1½lb eggs and packed them in her trousers then lay on a couch.

She was rewarded when fifteen lively emu chicks hatched out. Each is believed to have been worth £900 each.

— ∞ — ∞ — ∞ — ∞ — ∞ —

Faithful to the End

— ∞ — ∞ — ∞ — ∞ — ∞ —

QUITE remarkable was the attendance of 200 people at a ceremony marking the 50th anniversary of the death of a dog. It happened in Montana, United States.

Shep, a sheepdog, won his fame for waiting patiently for *five-and-a-half years* at a railway station for his dead master to return.

Not many ordinary humans can win such regard for sheer faithfulness.

— ∞ — ∞ — ∞ — ∞ — ∞ —

A West German Animal Protection Society say that owners who cycle to 'walk' their dogs are cruel. It makes it impossible for dogs to sniff around and cock their legs.

— ∞ — ∞ — ∞ — ∞ — ∞ —

The United States Post Office paid £475 to give Skippy, an alsatian shot by a postman, an elegant funeral service in the Los Angeles Pet Memorial Park.

Skippy was gunned down on Boxing Day as his owner went outside to give postman Floyd Sterling a Christmas present.

— ∞ — ∞ — ∞ — ∞ — ∞ —

A lovely story comes from New Zealand concerning a missing electronic wrist watch. The owner who lived in Auckland, thought at first he had mislaid the watch, then after three weeks gave it up as lost.

A day or so later however, he was woken up at 7am to hear the familiar twenty second interval bleep of the alarm of the watch. Another search commenced and at last, it was discovered that the sound was coming from deep inside his dog, Chaka, an old English Setter. As the animal had previously swallowed a disposable razor blade without apparent harm, they gave him laxatives this time to no avail.

Finally a vet induced the return of the watch, minus the leather strap. The watch had kept perfect time on its unusual journey. A watchdog indeed.

— ∞ — ∞ — ∞ — ∞ — ∞ —

And Now From Japan

— ∞ — ∞ — ∞ — ∞ — ∞ —

A pure white Japanese Akita puppy became the first of its breed to become a police dog in Britain recently, when it joined the West Midlands police force.

Recruited because of a shortage of German Shepherds, the breed most commonly used by the police, the seven-month-old puppy is similar in size and weight.

Often German Shepherds do not show a sufficiently stable temperament during the rigorous training procedures, a West Midlands police spokesman said, and some lack the necessary strength, courage or will to reach the high standards required of a police dog.

The Akita, named Santosha's Arashi Kumo but known as Rupert, was donated to the police by a pedigree breeder because one of his ears is the wrong shape, making him unsuitable for showing.

For the next five months he will learn the ropes at a Birmingham Police Station and will later join a full training course.

The Akita is the largest of the Japanese Spitz breeds and is used widely by police forces in Japan, where it is renowned for its courage.

— ∞ — ∞ — ∞ — ∞ — ∞ —

Donkeys are usually the most placid species of the animal world but there would appear to be an exception to every rule. A story comes from an Iranian village that trouble started when the owner of two donkeys tried to separate one from the other. One of the beasts refused to leave its mate and when the man tried to separate them, one flew at the man, bit his throat and killed him. The poor beast was beaten to death by the villagers.

— ∞ — ∞ — ∞ — ∞ — ∞ —

By the year 2000 it is forecast that Tanzania's 77,000 remaining elephants will have disappeared unless urgent action is taken against poachers. What a dreadful thought that these magnificent, dignified, great animals should be wiped out for the sheer greed of man.

— ∞ — ∞ — ∞ — ∞ — ∞ —

Five hundred wild goats have been slaughtered on the island of Aldabra in the Indian Ocean. The reason is that the rare tortoises on the island are being decimated as the goats destroy all the bushes which protect the 150,000 giant creatures from the intense heat.

— ∞ — ∞ — ∞ — ∞ — ∞ —

There is a story of a cat who had to be put on a crash diet when it was found that he was being fed seven breakfasts, seven lunches and seven dinners a day. Rejoicing in the name of Buster, this canny cat was fed unknowingly by seven different members of the staff when his owner was on holiday.

He mewed so piteously to each member of the staff that thinking he had not been fed, gave him food. He was wise enough only to approach them when they were alone, *never* when two or three were gathered together. Naturally like

Topsy, he grew and grew. Who thinks cats have no intelligence? Now his meals are strictly monitored.

— ∞ — ∞ — ∞ — ∞ — ∞ —

An East Anglian farmer who charged people 25p to see a six-legged cow was accused of 'sick exploitation' by the RSPCA.

Mr David Sadd saved the cow, which has two extra legs attached to her shoulders, from the slaughterhouse. He said it was a family pet and the charges paid for her food.

— ∞ — ∞ — ∞ — ∞ — ∞ —

Eighteen otters released into the wild in East Anglia in the past five years by the Otter Trust have all bred successfully. The Trust is now re-introducing otters into the River Stour in Dorset and also in Shropshire.

— ∞ — ∞ — ∞ — ∞ — ∞ —

A small terrier must have felt very tired when he decided to curl up and go to sleep – on of all places a busy railway line near Birmingham. The driver of a packed commuter train fortunately spotted him and stopped the train. He then went along but the terrier was not eager to wake up , and the driver then lifted him into his cab and handed him over to the police at the end of his journey.

— ∞ — ∞ — ∞ — ∞ — ∞ —

At Whitehaven, Cumbria, a hen settled into the cab of a taxi driver and was driven into town. The driver was in complete ignorance of his passenger, who apparently alighted in the town centre and began a stroll through the flower beds where she started to lay eggs.

— ∞ — ∞ — ∞ — ∞ — ∞ —

Six one-week-old owlets born recently at the New Forest Owl Sanctuary have been adopted by Jay, a springer spaniel. They nestle in under his head and he guards them with great affection. The barn owl population has been decreasing for some years and hand-reared owls are much sought after by estates which find them ideal to keep down rodents.

— ∞ — ∞ — ∞ — ∞ — ∞ —

The Arab Horse is the most ancient of all tamed horses, dating back as far as 5000BC. Every single grey on a race-course is descended from the Alcock Arabian.

— ∞ — ∞ — ∞ — ∞ — ∞ —

Edinburgh Zoo scored a great success in 1990 when they successfully overcame difficult problems and were able to show off *Mikumi*, a three-week-old rare White Rhino. The youngster was one of seven born. They were only the fourth in the world to be bred in captivity.

— ∞ — ∞ — ∞ — ∞ — ∞ —

Not only a rare animal, but it has a name which could well come from a fairy story, it was discovered by two youngsters in a bog in Bridlington, Yorkshire.

The Loopi-larf (a cross between a stoat and an owl) gets its name from the strange chuckling noise it makes when it feasts

211

on spiders' webs – its favourite food.

The strange creature was found by ten-year-old twins Hattie and Tom Bowler from Hastings. 'We were out hunting for slugs when we heard this strange giggling noise coming from the bog. When we looked closer we couldn't believe our eyes!'

An animal expert thinks this is a very important discovery. Only thirteen other Loopi-larfs have ever been sighted in the British Isles. We hope this find will be the first of many.

A bus near Sheffield had a surprise passenger, for when the vehicle pulled up at a regular stop, the first aboard was a Billy goat. He climbed to the top deck and despite all efforts refused to move. The driver took the bus to the depot where the goat was eventually led off to an animal sanctuary.

Cindy a cat took a nap on an armchair in Birmingham and awoke on the Isle of Wight when the removal van containing it arrived.

An orphaned baby seal stranded in a Somerset river was rescued by two policemen, who took him back to their police station at Taunton and put him in a cell under a shower.

The pup seemed to survive all right and was later taken to the RSPCA Wildlife Centre at Taunton and was doing well.

What other name could they bestow on him but 'Copper'.

— ∞ — ∞ — ∞ — ∞ — ∞ —

Animal psychologists cannot explain how some animals can find their way home from hundreds of miles away.

A classic case is that of Murka a black-and-white cat who was banned from her home in Moscow for unlatching the birdcage and killing two canaries. She was exiled to stay with the owners relations, some 400 miles away. However, she stayed in her new home just two days then disappeared.

It was a year after this that the cat's owner in Moscow noticed the cat near his apartment, it was Murka come home. Dirty, hungry, pregnant but otherwise unharmed, except the missing tip of her tail, were all humans could see for her 400-mile trek back home.

Let us hope she has given up killing canaries.

— ∞ — ∞ — ∞ — ∞ — ∞ —

What can we think of a racing pigeon that got blown off course in the storms of January 1990, and flew *7,600 miles*. It entitles the pigeon to a place in the *Guinness Book of Records*.

The four-year-old racing pigeon was released in the Shetland Isles to make the flight home in South Wales and ended up in China. In truth an incredible journey.

Its owners had given it up for lost when they received a letter from a Chinese fancier of Shanghai, who traced its origin to the Welsh Homing Union which in turn notified the owners. They have written to the gentleman saying that he is the new owner of the bird.

— ∞ — ∞ — ∞ — ∞ — ∞ —

There are several recorded cases of animals finding their way back to their homes over incredible distances, but the instance of the white Husky Alaskan sled dog is quite amazing.

The dog disappeared when the plane carrying its owner crashed in Alaska along the Soviet coast. The animal, lost and injured, eventually found its way back to the place where the plane started, by travelling over freezing snowy wastes, a distance of over 250 miles

— ∞ — ∞ — ∞ — ∞ — ∞ —

Surely Minette's Ninth Life!

— ∞ — ∞ — ∞ — ∞ — ∞ —

WHEN a six-month-old cat has already expended several of her lives on an 8,560 mile voyage by raft, she can reasonably expect to be received on dry land with a degree of acclamation. But black-and-white Minette was to all intents and purposes clapped into irons and given a death sentence when she landed in Australia a year or so ago.

Her raft, La Balsa, with its four-man crew made land near Brisbane after a voyage of five months duration. Health officials seized Minette, put her in a cage, placed her in quarantine, and passed sentence of death within twenty-four hours because she came from Ecuador where the dread disease rabies was prevalent.

Captain Vital Alsar, Spanish-Mexican skipper of the raft, said that they had set out with four cats and four parrots and Minette was the only survivor. Indeed, she had been washed overboard many times, but members of the crew dived into the sea and rescued her. The Australian authorities were, however, adamant in their resolve that Minette must die, and the pleadings of the crew seemed of no avail. The *Sunday Express* in Brisbane reported that hope had almost been given up when Captain Charles Helleman of the 8,000 ton Swedish cargo ship, *Cirrus*, joined the fray and declared that he would willingly have the cat on his ship rather than see her destroyed as a prohibited immigrant.

The port officials relented and permitted the cat to board the *Cirrus*, with instructions that she was not to be allowed out of her cage until the ship was outside territorial waters. Captain Helleman agreed and promised that they would either give Minette a home until the crew of the raft wanted her back, when they would drop her off at the nearest port, or they would keep her with them on the high seas for the rest of her life. And as this is surely her last life it is to be hoped that the cargo ship proves more comfortable and less hazardous than La Balsa.

Minette deserves her good fortune, for under Captain Alsar she had helped to prove that it was possible for ancient man to have voyaged from South America to the other side of the world by raft. The other members of the crew were Marc Modena, a Frenchman, at forty-three the oldest member of the expedition, Gabriel Salas of Chile, and Norman Tetreault, a Canadian.

— ∞ — ∞ — ∞ — ∞ — ∞ —

A Donkey Serenade

WAS Zooloo an intelligent donkey? She forgot her calling card and chose the wrong time to call anyway. Whether she took people 'for a ride' on her own initiative or whether someone took her for a ride as a prank has never been discovered, but the fact remains that at 2.30 one morning the occupants of an apartment house in Statten

Island, New York City, were awakened to the braying of a donkey.

Mr Giovinazza had arrived home from a bowling alley around midnight and there was no sign of a donkey then. He went to bed and to sleep, but twice woke up hearing strange noises. Thinking he had been dreaming, it was not until he was awakened for the third time that he actually got up and looked into the hallway. He still thought he was dreaming, for there looking at him and starting to mount the stairs was a 350lb donkey. Realising at last that this was a real live intruder, he telephoned the police, who decided it was a job for the American Society for the Prevention of Cruelty to Animals.

The officer on duty responded to the call but on arrival decided he needed help, so he called the ASPCA manager, Mr Hollinde. Meanwhile neighbours and volunteer helpers had forgathered and, like crowds the world over, were excelling themselves in giving free advice on how to coax Zooloo from the apartment house on to the street. For half an hour the two men from the ASPCA did all they knew to get the donkey to move. They pushed and pulled, they bribed with carrots, apples and bread, and finally they succeeded. The next problem was to get her into their van, but a prime specimen like Zooloo would not fit into the one they had brought, so a larger truck had to be sent for. Meanwhile the adventurer was tied to a fire hydrant.

The truck arrived and then they began pushing, pulling and bribing all over again. As dawn broke the donkey was successfully loaded, and for two days was housed at the Society's home enjoying meals of apples and grain, whilst they tried to find a home for her.

The story had a happy ending. At a donkey stables some two miles from Mr Giovinazza's apartment, the owner counting heads realised that one called Zooloo was missing. But the mystery of how she strayed two miles remains unsolved. Unless she went under her own power, it would have taken two hefty fellows to get her there, even had they used the encouragement the ASPCA found only partially effective, a bunch of carrots.

— ∞ — ∞ — ∞ — ∞ — ∞ —

After flying thousands of miles across the Atlantic Ocean, a rare bird from Canada reached Britain safely, only to meet its death by crashing into the plate glass door of Slimbridge Bird Sanctuary in Gloucestershire. It is believed to be the first sighting of a grey-cheeked thrush in Britain.

— ∞ — ∞ — ∞ — ∞ — ∞ —

An elephant calf was killed by a passenger train in India and caused chaos. The scream of the youngster brought a herd of elephants rushing to the accident. They sat round the body as it died and refused to be dislodged.

The train crew were forced to take the train back to its starting point Mettupalayam, 1,162 miles south of New Delhi.

— ∞ — ∞ — ∞ — ∞ — ∞ —

Chinese police arrested 203 people for hunting the endangered Giant Panda. They recovered 148 pelts, representing about one in seven of the 1,000 pandas alive at the last count, said the World Wide Fund for Nature.

— ∞ — ∞ — ∞ — ∞ — ∞ —

A fisherman whose dog vanished as it swam across the Pechora river in Northern Siberia, later caught a 6ft long pike, and noticed a tail sticking out of its jaws. He cut the fish open and the dog struggled out, barking, and none the worse for its experience, Moscow Radio claimed.

— ∞ — ∞ — ∞ — ∞ — ∞ —

Two policemen used an improvised lasso to rope a swan which mistook the M3 near Basingstoke, Hants, for a river and crash-landed in the fast lane. It was released in a nearby pond.

— ∞ — ∞ — ∞ — ∞ — ∞ —

A labrador called Hutch had to have his photograph taken in a booth before British Rail officials would issue the owner with his season ticket!

— ∞ — ∞ — ∞ — ∞ — ∞ —

An 18ft whale was shepherded back out to sea by RSPCA officers and coastguards after running aground in the Bristol Channel below the M4 road bridge.

— ∞ — ∞ — ∞ — ∞ — ∞ —

A couple in Gloucestershire hired a car for a month because a robin had laid its eggs in the engine of their Range Rover.

— ∞ — ∞ — ∞ — ∞ — ∞ —

Fortunately the cruelty which is practised on so many animals also has a brighter side, thanks largely due to conservationist lobbies.

In Cornwall recently badgers living alongside a new £7 million road found their territory cut in half – and this would have meant them crossing the road, with the inevitable high death toll. The road builders have built a Badger Subway to enable them to travel safely between their setts and feeding grounds.

Sweep, the two-year-old pet mongrel belonging to a Staff Nurse in West Cumbria was knocked down by a lorry and seemed dead, his heart had stopped beating. His mistress, however, in desperation gave him the kiss of life and the lucky dog recovered.

Amorous male toads use the Westcountry roads for their perambulations to find females, and hundreds are killed as they make their way from their normal habitat to the ponds where the females are likely to be found. Because the movement of toads is fairly predictable several crossings were set up for them, some manned by conservationists. Unfortunately in the dark they are rarely avoided as they look like stones on the highway.

— ∞ — ∞ — ∞ — ∞ — ∞ —

150 pilot whales, some 20ft long 'committed suicide' on a remote Falklands beach, and all attempts to persuade even the smallest to return to the sea failed.

— ∞ — ∞ — ∞ — ∞ — ∞ —

A motorway near Rochester had to be closed to enable police to coax a grounded swan into taking off.

— ∞ — ∞ — ∞ — ∞ — ∞ —

Coastguards saved the life of a dolphin stranded in shallow waters off Littlehampton, Sussex, by taking it to a lifeboat station by Land Rover and releasing it in deep water.

— ∞ — ∞ — ∞ — ∞ — ∞ —

A hedgehog climbed into a car's suspension in Cornwall and travelled 350 miles to Nottingham. It arrived unhurt and was only found when the car driver stopped and heard squeaks coming from the front of the car.

— ∞ — ∞ — ∞ — ∞ — ∞ —

Firemen rescued two donkeys from the roof of a restaurant at Deal, near Sevenoaks, Kent, after the animals, whose field is on the same level as the roof, wandered on to it, looking for food, and became stuck.

— ∞ — ∞ — ∞ — ∞ — ∞ —

A prize was awarded at an English pet show to the dog who wagged his tail the fastest.

— ∞ — ∞ — ∞ — ∞ — ∞ —

Dodie Smith, the author, who died in 1990 and was famous for the fascinating film *One Hundred and One Dalmatians*, left £2,000 in her will for the utmost protection and care of her own dalmatian, Charlie.

The dog however died just six months before his owner who was ninety-four years of age. The bequest therefore became part of the author's £472,000 estate.

Dodie Smith, in leaving the money for Charlie, said she did so because dogs and dalmatians in particular had been a source of inspiration and income for her.

— ∞ — ∞ — ∞ — ∞ — ∞ —

We have heard of the amorous human male, but different is the story which comes from Jamma, India.

A large monkey became very amorous and finding his way to a hospital went from bed to bed kissing and hugging some thirty women patients.

The lovelorn animal was eventually caught and caged for sixty-six days and it was then that the authorities decided he should be shot after his victims complained long and bitterly and the nurses threatened to go on strike.

Devout Hindoos however protested that the animal should be saved. So it was released on the edge of a forest by wildlife officials. As it jumped from tree to tree, thousands of people gathered to give it a fond farewell and it soon disappeared from view, perhaps to seek a mate of its own species.

— ∞ — ∞ — ∞ — ∞ — ∞ —

Useful Addresses

— ∞ — ∞ — ∞ — ∞ — ∞ —

Animal Aid Society
7 Castle Street
Tonbridge
Kent TN9 1BH

Animal Medical Center
510 East 62nd Street
New York
10021

British Mule Society
Mrs Travis
Hope Mount Farm
Top of Hope
Astonfield
Nr Ashbourne
Derbyshire DE6 2FR

Donkey Sanctuary
Sidmouth
Devon
EX10 0NU

Hearing Dogs for the Deaf Training Centre
London Road
Lewknor
Oxford
OX9 5RY

Help for the Disabled
Brook House
1 Lower Lodges
Kenilworth
Warks
CV8 2GN

International Fund for Animal Welfare
Tubwell House
New Road
Crowborough
East Sussex
TN6 2QH

London Wildlife Trust
80 York Way
London
N1 9AG

National Shire Horse Centre
Dunstone
Yealmpton
Plymouth
PL8 2EL

New Forest Owl Sanctuary
Crow Lane
Crow
Ringwood
Hants

Petwatch
PO Box 16
Brighouse
W Yorks
HD6 1DS

Reptile Collection Trust
College Gates
2 Deansway
Worcester
WR1 2JD

RSPCA Head Office
The Causeway
Horsham
West Sussex
RH12 1HG

Seal Sanctuary
Gweek
Cornwall